Yes, You Can Time the Market!

Yes, You Can
Time the Market!

Ben Stein and Phil DeMuth

WILEY

JOHN WILEY & SONS, INC.

Published by John Wiley & Sons, Inc., Hoboken, New Jersey.
Published simultaneously in Canada.

For general information on our other products and services please contact our
Customer Care Department within the United States at (800) 762-2974, outside the
United States at (317) 572-3993 or fax (317) 572-4002.

Wiley also publishes its books in a variety of electronic formats. Some content that
appears in print may not be available in electronic books. For more information about
Wiley products, visit our Web site at www.wiley.com.

Library of Congress Cataloging-in-Publication Data:

Stein, Ben, 1947–
  Yes, you can time the market! / Ben Stein, Phil DeMuth.
     p.   cm.
  Includes bibliographical references and index.
  ISBN 0-471-43016-1 (cloth)
  1. Stock price forecasting.   2. Speculation.   3. Investment analysis.
  I. DeMuth, Phil, 1950–   II. Title.
  HG4637.S737 2003
  332.63'2042—dc21

                                                          2002156151

Printed in the United States of America.

10   9   8   7   6   5   4   3   2

For Alex and Julia

Preface

Yes, You Can Time the Market! grew out of a series of lunch conversations between the authors at the Piazza Rodeo in Beverly Hills and on the bike path in Santa Monica in 1997 to 2000. Ben Stein insisted that the stock market was too high. Phil DeMuth countered that, while it might *seem* high, this was an opinion without practical significance. As everyone knew, ". . . you cannot time the market. . . ." During the palmy days of the unending bull market, there was no need for Market Timing. It was simple enough to just buy a stock or a mutual fund that was heading for Neptune and go along for the ride. Then the stock market started dropping like an anvil off a cliff, and the subject merited closer investigation. How had people come to accept the notion that the price of the market was irrelevant, when price applied so ruthlessly everywhere else?

There was this to consider: The field of Market Timing had become the province of short-term fortune-telling cranks, which gave the whole endeavor an unsavory reputation. When analyzed, their typical investment strategy fell apart like a cheap suit, making them easy targets for finance experts to set up and then demolish.

But when we shifted to the long term, the data revealed that fundamental stock market valuation metrics clearly showed when the market was over- or underpriced. All that we had to do was use the tools of technical analysis—the chart and the moving average—and add to them fundamental criteria like the dividend yield or the price/earnings ratio. It seemed astonishing that Wall Street, with all its MBAs and high-priced talent, had missed something so obvious. Possibly this was because these measures tell us nothing constructive about where the stock market will be tomorrow or next month, but only years from now. They were not short-term selling tools.

If the stock market can be said to be priced high or low for an investor with a long-term perspective, then it follows that there are better and worse times to buy and sell stocks. We hope this book helps you find them. It summarizes a colossal amount of data, and we hope to have scored some runs and hits along with any errors. More broadly, we hope that it will re-open the debate on the usefulness of Market Timing to investors everywhere.

BEN STEIN
PHIL DEMUTH

About the Authors

BEN STEIN has had one of the most diverse careers known to man. He is the son of the world-famous economist and policy advisor, Herbert Stein. He received a BA with honors in economics from Columbia in 1966, and worked as an economist for the Department of Commerce. In 1967, he entered Yale Law School and graduated as valedictorian of his class in 1970. While at Yale, he studied corporate finance under distinguished professors Henry Wallich and James Tobin. Ben Stein is known to many as a movie and television personality, especially from *Ferris Bueller's Day Off* and from his long-running quiz show, *Win Ben Stein's Money*. But he has probably worked more at personal and corporate finance than at any other subject. He has written about finance for *Barron's* and the *Wall Street Journal* for decades. He was one of the chief busters of the junk bond frauds of the 1980s, has been a long-time critic of corporate executives' self-dealing, and has written two self-help books about personal finance. He frequently travels the country speaking about finance (www.benstein.com).

PHIL DEMUTH was valedictorian of his class at the University of California at Santa Barbara in 1972. He went on for his masters in communication and doctorate in clinical psychology. A psychologist with a longstanding interest in the stock market, he has written for the *Wall Street Journal* and *Barron's* as well as *Human Behavior* and *Psychology Today.* His opinions have been quoted on *theStreet.com* and *Fortune* magazine. He is a registered investment advisor and president of Conservative Wealth Management in Los Angeles, California (www.phildemuth.com).

Contents

Yes, You Can
Time the Market!

Chapter One

The Impossibility of
Market Timing

"You can't time the market." This a well-known shibboleth, among the most basic tenets of serious stock market investors from Nobel Prize winning economists to your basic corner stock brokers. You cannot in advance tell when the market is going to go up or down based on some already known data. That is supposedly fundamental.

Just listen to the voices:

From David Swensen, chief investment officer of the mighty Yale University endowment, short and sweet: "Serious investors avoid timing markets."

From Mr. Swensen's close friend, investment manager and frequent commentator Charles Ellis: "There is no evidence of any large institutions having anything like consistent ability to get in when the market is low and get out when the market is high."

From one of our favorite commentators on stock market investing, William J. Bernstein, in his *Four Pillars of Investing:* the results of financial services and insurance companies picking times to buy stocks are and were ". . . awful . . . the performance of market timing newsletters . . . was even worse. . . ."

From William F. Sharpe, Nobel Prize winner, and his essay, "Likely Gains From Market Timing": ". . . a manager . . . should probably avoid market timing altogether. . . ."

From a seer named Larry E. Swedroe in his book, *What Wall Street Doesn't Want You to Know:* The odds against market timing are ". . . huge. . . ." Mr. Swedroe cites an article in *Fortune* of May 12, 1997 to the same effect: "No one knows where the market is going . . . That's the simple truth." (Although, as Mr. Swedroe points out, that does not stop *Fortune* from trying to show that it does.)

John Bogle, one of the smartest and most capable investment gurus of all time, head of the Vanguard family of funds for many years, says flatly: "Indeed, my impression is that trying to do market timing is likely, not only not to add value to your investment program, but to be counterproductive."

Really?

How can this possibly be?

Market Timing is the concept that there are some times when indicators that can be read at the time say it is a better time to buy or sell than other times. Market Timing is the notion that an investor can look at certain data and have an idea, a good idea, that the market is overpriced or underpriced and is likely to go down or go up.

Now, at one level, it is simply preposterous to say that there should be and can be no Market Timing. After all, what moves the market every second of every day is a huge number of buyers and sellers deciding to buy or sell, sometimes buy *and* sell, that day. Usually, though far from always, they are buying individual stocks. But on many other occasions, they are buying indices or baskets of stocks second by second, altogether by the billions of shares every day.

In the aggregate, what is happening every day is that the mass of investors and speculators are Market Timing every second of every day. Obviously, they are making decisions about what to buy and sell and when to sell and buy it. This is, in itself, Market Timing.

Every day, when the stock market goes down on poor earnings rumors, or goes up on rumors of future rate cuts by the Federal Reserve, the traders are timing the market, guessing that now is a better time to buy or sell than some other time. So in a way, it makes no sense to say that Market Timing is not a helpful strategy or that no smart person does it—unless we were to say that the great bulk of investors are not smart. This may be true, but then we would have to go further and say that no one who traded on any day was smart or experienced, and that is saying too much.

Moreover, what about all of those clever hedge fund managers? They mostly make money by buying and by doing something only some of us ever do, selling short. But they often trade frequently, blindingly more so than the individual Ma-and-Pa Kettle investor at home in Smallville. Every time they buy or sell short indices or exchange traded funds, they are timing the market, even if sometimes only over a very short time. Yet, this, too, is Market Timing. Are all of these people fools? Some of them make pretty good returns for fools.

Then there is a factor standing in the way of the Anti-Market Timers that is about as big as Gibraltar. If Market Timing is futile and meaninglessly foolish, then what about the basic concept of price? How can price be meaningless in terms of stocks, while it is meaningful everywhere else?

This is a crucial question, and it is the one that began us on this project. If price means something in terms of real estate or oil futures or bonds or cars or shirts, how can it be meaningless in terms of stocks? If there is a price that is a "high" price for an apartment building relative to its rental income, can it be that there is no such thing as a "high" or "low" price of a share of stock in terms of its dividends or earnings or book value or some other metric—maybe even in terms of its usual price? If natural gas is high or low in relation to coal or oil, can it be that stocks are not high or low relative to other investment classes or to their own earnings or dividends? Does the basic principle that price is king in markets have no application in stocks?

Supposedly, price tells us the supreme wisdom of the markets at any given moment in time, since it is the synthesis of all of the available data about a stock's prospects at any given moment. But we know that price changes on a dime; price is like a hummingbird constantly maneuvering and changing position in the universe. Can it be that the price is unattached even over long periods to any kind of gravity of earnings or book value or past prices of the stock or of markets generally? Can it possibly be that a stock price is simply a totally random artifact not connected with anything else on earth? In that case, why have prices at all?

But if price does matter in relation to shares of stock, as it does in everything else on earth—including labor—then how can it be that all prices are of equal predictive value? Is there not some number that will, over long periods at least, tell us the likely course of stock price movements? If we can be fairly sure that a rental apartment property that is selling for a much higher multiple of rental revenues than it ever has in the past is poised to fall, or is at least less likely to go up greatly than when it was cheaper, why is the same thing not true for stocks?

Or, to put it as simply as possible, we asked ourselves, could it possibly be that there is no such thing as "cheap" or "expensive" when one talks about buying or selling stocks, but there is for everything else on earth? And if shares of stock can be cheap or expensive, cannot markets themselves, the aggregate of all stocks, be cheap or expensive? And if they can be cheap or expensive, does this not have some presumptive value about the likelihood of stocks going up or down?

Asking ourselves these questions led to our preliminary research. We looked at years in which the earnings yield of stocks—the amount the total Standard & Poor's 500 earned as a numerator and the price of the aggregate S&P 500 as the denominator—was abnormally low, say below 5 percent (that translates to a price/earnings ratio of 20 or above) and calculated how well the market had done 5, 10, and 20 years afterward in the postwar period. We then compared those gains or losses with similar periods in which the beginning point showed stocks to be "cheap," namely when the earnings yield was above 10 percent, or a price/earnings ratio of 10 or below. We found that in general, over long periods of time, gains were starkly higher if the beginning point showed stocks to be "cheaper" in terms of having a higher yield of earnings.

This led us to make much more extensive studies of the effects of buying stocks when they were "cheap" or "expensive" by a series of other metrics. The results were quite consistent. The prices of stocks indeed could not be timed (at least, not by us) in any meaningful way in the short run. Price movements were more or less random over periods of months and even of a year or more. They were not closely connected with other metrics we could find.

But in the long run, over many years, the "cheapness" or "expensiveness" of stocks by the measure of earnings yield, dividend yield, price-to-book value, even to the usual moving average of the price, had a great deal to do with superior results in terms of return on investment. Investing in stocks generally in this past century has been a good thing to do over long periods. But we found that buying when stocks were "cheap" led to far higher returns than when they were "expensive." By any of several measurements, total long-term return on stocks was greatly enhanced by "timing" the market, or buying when stocks as a group looked to be cheap. Returns over long periods were still good if the investor bought consistently no matter whether stocks were high or low by our measurements. But they were far better if the investor bought when shares were at certain buying points suggested by their price relative to other easily ascertainable numbers.

In the chapters that follow, we show how Market Timing turned out relative to simply (and not foolishly) buying consistently month-by-month for a period of decades. We think the results are startling. We also point out how some degree of measurement of stock prices, coupled with an attempt to buy when stocks are cheaper rather than more expensive, can save investors from genuine catastrophes over the shorter run (and remember that, as Mr. Keynes said, "In the long run, we are all dead"). We discuss which of our measurements yielded the best buying results.

Then we discuss why for most of the twentieth century clever people could manipulate the data to make it seem as if Market Timing did not work. *Hint:* It all has to do with who is picking the beginning and ending points. We then attempt an analysis of what role *macro* factors such as earnings growth or shrinkage, long- or short-term, interest rates, dividend levels, bond rates, and other interest rates play in exactly why timing the market in the simple ways we suggest works so well.

Or, we should say, we talk about why Market Timing has worked so well over the past century. It is always possible that we are in new territory and playing by new rules that render all previous guidance obsolete. But usually belief in a "new paradigm" goes before an immense fall. The past is an imperfect guide, but it is the best—and only—one we have.

Have a look at what we say and draw your own conclusions.

One note in the beginning: Have we lived by our own rules? Do we eat our own cooking? Yes. How have the results been? Not by any means perfect, but a whole lot better than if we had not invested by them. We have made some money in a very difficult investment climate using these rules. Much more important, we have avoided *losing* a great deal of money by following these rules, at least so far. The future is another country, but we have history on our side. We do not claim these tools will make you rich overnight. They definitely will not help you make a fortune in the short run and they will not make you a fortune in the long run unless you *consistently* invest a lot of money by them. We certainly do not claim that this is "black box" rocket science. This book is just about the enduring power of price and letting it save you from a myriad of problems.

But that is not a small thing. Warren Buffett likes to say that the number one rule of making money is not to lose money and the second rule is to remember the first rule. We would add a further thought: In investing and in handling money generally, the key is not to do anything genuinely brilliant and to avoid doing something really stupid. We hope this book helps. It has certainly helped us.

Chapter Two

The Power of Price

Throughout this book, we continuously reference the Standard & Poor's 500 Index. Standard & Poor's (S&P) is a company that specializes in financial analysis, and their index seeks to include the 500 leading stocks from the leading industries in the United States. Over a trillion investment dollars are currently pegged to this index of large companies, which often serves as a representation of the U.S. stock market as a whole. We use the S&P Index because we have no claim to be able to pick stocks individually. Exhaustive research shows that almost no one else does either. In our opinion, buying large indices is so clearly the preferred way to invest in stocks that we do not even suggest using timing on individual stocks unless you have been following a stock closely for a long time and are clairvoyant. Figure 2.1 shows how the S&P 500 fared over the twentieth century.

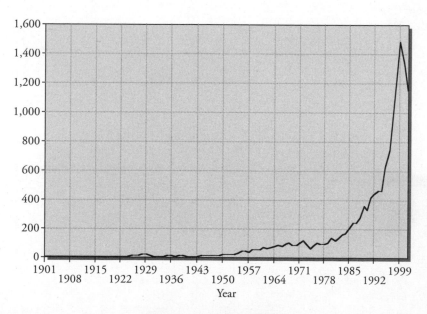

Figure 2.1   S&P 500

The S&P closed out 1902 at 8, and ended 2001 at 1148—an impressive run. But recall that these numbers have not been adjusted for inflation. Remember when candy bars cost a nickel? If we take inflation out of the picture, we get what is called the *real* S&P, meaning *adjusted for inflation.* We will be using these inflation-adjusted figures throughout the book, backfiguring everything in terms of 2001 dollars. Transformed to this 2001-dollar scale, the S&P 500 looks like Figure 2.2.

Now the first half of the century shows up on the board, while allowing the incredible run up of the late 1990s its due. The performance of the stock market has been nothing short of astonishing. But it has not been continuously good every year, a point we get to in more detail shortly.

There is one concept we need to explain before going further, and that is the *moving average.* An average is created when a series of numbers is summed and then divided by as many as were added. A moving average plots an average as it changes over time,

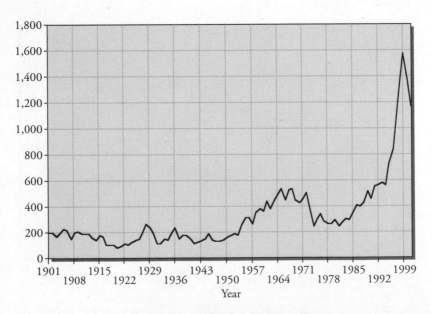

Figure 2.2   The Real S&P 500

with each new point adding the newest information and dropping the oldest. For the year 1902, we could plot a point that averaged where the S&P 500 had been from 1887 to 1902. For 1903, we could update this year by plotting a point averaging the S&P from 1888 to 1903. The next year, we could average 1889 to 1904, and so on. Figure 2.3 graphs the price of the real S&P 500 over the past century once more, but this time superimposes a 15-year moving average on top of it. The moving average is the thin line snaking through the thick line. Sometimes the S&P 500 is above this long-term trend line, while at other times it is below.

There is nothing magical about choosing the 15-year moving average as a point of comparison. We could just as easily have created a 10-year moving average or a 20-year moving average. It is merely a way of showing where the S&P 500 Index stands at any given time compared to its long-term trend. Just to be consistent, we will use the 15-year moving average as our benchmark of

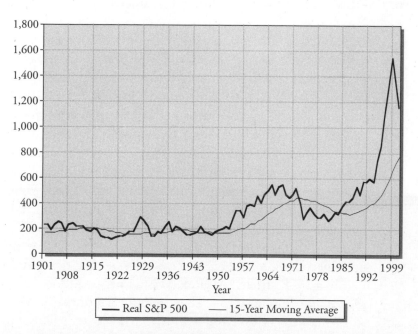

Figure 2.3   Real S&P 500 with 15-Year Moving Average

comparison throughout the book. Even though it is arbitrary, it is nevertheless extremely important.

Why? All of us judge the value we receive for the price we pay by intuitively comparing the current price with what historically we are used to paying. If we have been paying $1,000 a month in rent for the past three years, and now our landlord wants to charge us $3,000, we bridle because we sense that this is high. If we go to the gas pump and find gas selling for 50 cents a gallon, we smile because that gas price is cheap compared with what it was. The point of this book—so simple that a child can grasp it, yet so elusive that your broker will never get it—is that you are better off buying cheap. The 15-year moving average allows us to tell when stocks are cheap or expensive in historical terms. It is a continuous accounting for historical costs.

Let's be fair: The idea that what is low might go up and what is high might come down is not a new one. Researchers have studied this phenomenon with individual stocks:

- DeBondt and Thaler wrote an article in 1985 for the *Journal of Finance* titled "Does the Stock Market Overreact?" They looked at the best- and worst-performing stocks over the previous five years for every year from 1932 to 1977, and compared the subsequent performance of these stocks to that of the New York Stock Exchange as a whole. What did they find? The best-performing stocks over the previous five years averaged a performance 6 percentage points below that of the total exchange in the year and a half following, while the worst performing stocks ended up beating the market by 18 percentage points during this same period.
- Poterba and Summers (the Larry Summers who later went on to become secretary of the treasury) extended these findings in a 1988 article, "Mean Reversion in Stock Prices, Evidence and Implications." They examined returns from 17 stock markets all over the world from 1926 to 1985, and found that, over the long term, high returns are followed by

low returns, and low returns are followed by high returns. Their recommendation: Buy securities that have recently suffered significant price declines.

- Power, Lonie, and Lonie studied stocks in the United Kingdom and derived the same conclusion. In "The Over-Reaction Effect—Some U.K. Evidence," they reported that the 30 stocks with the worst investment performance from 1973 to 1982 went on to trounce the 30 stocks with the best performance from that period (as well as the market as a whole) from 1983 to 1987.

If price—measured in various ways—could be a significant factor in selecting individual stocks, why not apply it to an index of the stock market as a whole? Yet if it made sense to speak of the market *price* as being high or low, that meant that *every* time was not an equally good buying occasion. Some times would be better than others—possibly much better. In other words, other things being equal, we would want to buy when the market was priced low.

For the present, let us do something simple: Let us define low as being when stocks are selling below their long-term average. In Figure 2.3, that means when the thick line (the price) is below the thin line (the long-term trend). This does not happen every day, but it does happen. In later chapters, we discuss other yardsticks to measure how cheaply or expensively the stock market is priced.

Suppose we buy stocks only when the market is below the 15-year trend. Here we have Market Timing at its most basic, its most primitive: using the raw price of the stock market as our only guide by comparing the current price with its long-term average. That is, imagine that a Market Timer considered nothing more than the price of the stock market when making his purchases throughout the past century. Could something this obvious, this banal, possibly have been of any value?

To find out, we looked at where the market stood at the end of each year for the last 100 years. We then measured whether this was above or below the 15-year moving average: the long-term mean of where the price had been heading up to that time. If it were above this line, we considered that stocks were selling at a premium. Below its long-term trend line, we thought stocks were on sale. We put the years into two piles, accordingly: expensive (Buy High) and cheap (Buy Low).

Next, we added up what would have happened if we bought the stocks at the end of all of the *Buy High* years and held them for various time periods: 5, 10, 15, and 20 years. For our first Buy High year, 1902, we assume we bought the S&P Index at that time and added up where our stocks would have been at the end of 1907, 1912, 1917, and 1922. Our next Buy High year was 1903, so we looked at the performance of the market from then until 1908, 1913, 1918, and 1923. We went through the whole century, seeing how every one of these Buy High years did 5, 10, 15, and 20 years later. Then we averaged these returns by time period: all the 5-year returns, all the 10-year returns, all the 15-year returns, and all the 20-year returns.

We did the same thing for all the *Buy Low* years. For our first year, 1907, we saw how stocks purchased with a cost basis from the end of that year performed at the end of 1912, 1917, 1922, and 1927. The next year when we thought stocks might be attractively priced was 1913, so we examined the hypothetical returns that would have followed had we purchased stocks then and sold them at the end of 1918, 1923, 1928, and 1933. We went through the entire century in this fashion, and then averaged the total returns by each holding period: 5, 10, 15, and 20 years.

Figure 2.4 plots the outcomes of these two investment strategies, buying high versus buying low throughout the century, and shows how well each approach worked over the subsequent time periods.

These outcomes are *total real returns,* which is to say that they are adjusted for inflation and assume that all dividends over the period were reinvested back into the market. We use total real returns as our benchmark throughout the book. Be aware that they

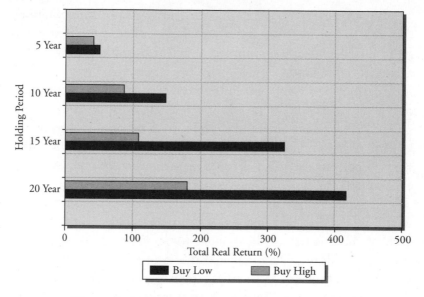

Figure 2.4   Lump Sum Investing, 1902–2001

do not tell the whole story, however, because they are not adjusted for transaction fees (taxes, management fees, and commissions).

In every case, the investor who bought low has a better total real return than the investor who bought high.

Not only that, but the spread widens over time. No wonder most Market Timers have been getting it wrong. *Market Timing is most frequently used as a short-term tactic, when it is really best suited to a long-term investment strategy.* This suits our purposes fine, because we want to help the long-term, conservative investor, not the nervous day trader with his coffee and cigarettes and his eyeballs glued to the flashing quotes on his computer screen.

At five years, buying the market when the price of stocks was below its mean averaged a 9 percent annualized total real return. Buying when the price of stocks was above its mean earned a 5 percent annualized total real return. Remember a basic truth from Statistics 101: A 9 percent return is not 4 percent better than a 5 percent return, it is 4 percentage points *more* but 80 percent *better*.

Was this a fluke? We decided to measure not only whether the price of the S&P 500 Index was above or below the long-term trend line, but also *how far* it was above or below this moving average. In other words, how high or low it was.

We dropped each year into one of four categories (called *quartiles*) depending on how far it was above or below the moving average compared to the others. The top 25 percent of all years we labeled *High,* the next 25 percent we labeled *Above Average,* the next 25 percent we called *Below Average,* and the bottom 25 percent we called *Low.*

We looked at all the years in each quartile and measured what would have happened had we bought the stocks at the end of each of these years and held them for exactly 20 years—a nice long-term holding. We calculated the total real returns for every year and then averaged them for each quartile. The results are shown in Figure 2.5. We discovered that the more we paid, the worse our total returns; the less we paid, the better we liked our long-term results.

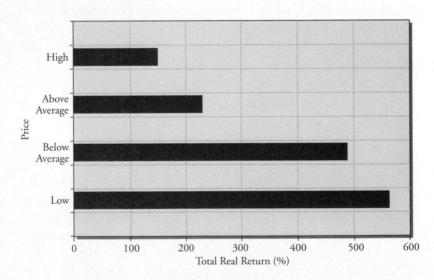

**Figure 2.5   Twenty-Year Total Real Return by
Price Quartile, 1902–2001**

How odd. The price of stocks when purchased seemed to have a decisive effect on our investment returns. But Wall Street has been saying: You cannot time the market; buy stocks today, regardless of price, since stocks always go up in the long run. Our findings are exactly the opposite, and yet they agree perfectly with everyday experience. Far from being an irrelevant factor that we should dismiss from our minds when purchasing stocks, price appears to be an extraordinarily important factor that we ignore at our peril.

Table 2.1 shows the relative price of the market by our price-sensitive criterion for each of the last hundred years, and the subsequent returns issuing from them. Price here is divided into the same quartiles just described: High (top 25 percent), Above (the 15-year Moving) Average, Below (the 15-year Moving) Average, and Low (bottom 25 percent).

Consider the discipline that purchasing stocks on this regimen would have placed on you. You would have been buying stocks during World War I and the early 1920s, while avoiding the new era investment boom of the late 1920s. You would have bought stocks throughout the Great Depression and World War II and its aftermath. Apart from reinvesting the dividends, you would not have bought a single share during the 1950s or 1960s, but you would have jumped in again in the 1970s and early 1980s. The last year you would have bought stocks during the twentieth century was 1984.

People familiar with the history of Wall Street will be aware that this is exactly the opposite of what everyone else was doing. Buying low is a *contrarian* investment philosophy. Most people get excited about stocks during bull markets, the most recent example being the Internet/Telecom bubble of the late 1990s. Everywhere you went, people were bragging about how much they made off Qualcomm and Yahoo! and other high fliers of the period. The results over this period until late 2002 have been tragic.

When the public gets excited about the stock market, stock prices get bid up to stratospheric levels, making them too expensive

Table 2.1 Total Real Returns Following Year Invested

Year	Price	+5 Years (%)	+10 Years (%)	+15 Years (%)	+20 Years (%)
1902	High	−11	45	0	43
1903	Above Average	51	51	22	69
1904	High	32	11	−2	64
1905	High	4	27	−33	75
1906	High	5	20	−16	97
1907	Below Average	64	12	61	305
1908	High	0	−19	12	310
1909	High	−16	−26	24	229
1910	Above Average	22	−36	68	186
1911	Above Average	14	−21	87	72
1912	Below Average	−31	−2	148	67
1913	Low	−19	12	311	186
1914	Low	−12	48	291	189
1915	Below Average	−47	38	135	209
1916	Low	−30	64	51	318
1917	Low	43	261	143	315
1918	Low	38	409	254	439
1919	Low	67	342	227	409
1920	Low	163	346	488	472
1921	Low	135	116	498	257
1922	Low	152	69	189	204
1923	Low	268	156	290	269
1924	Below Average	165	96	205	242
1925	Above Average	70	124	118	266
1926	Above Average	−8	154	52	147
1927	High	−33	15	21	72
1928	High	−30	6	0	19
1929	High	−26	15	29	58
1930	High	32	28	115	143
1931	Below Average	177	65	168	355
1932	Below Average	71	80	155	426
1933	Above Average	52	44	71	240
1934	Below Average	56	75	114	443

Table 2.1   *(Continued)*

Year	Price	+5 Years (%)	+10 Years (%)	+15 Years (%)	+20 Years (%)
1935	Above Average	−3	64	84	399
1936	High	−40	−3	65	297
1937	Below Average	5	49	208	450
1938	Above Average	−5	12	124	473
1939	Below Average	12	37	248	540
1940	Below Average	68	89	413	613
1941	Low	63	176	565	1,022
1942	Low	42	193	422	812
1943	Below Average	19	136	505	804
1944	Below Average	22	210	470	793
1945	High	13	205	324	639
1946	Below Average	70	309	590	729
1947	Low	107	268	544	933
1948	Low	99	410	662	974
1949	Below Average	154	367	630	670
1950	Above Average	171	277	556	518
1951	High	141	306	388	485
1952	High	78	212	400	473
1953	High	156	283	440	358
1954	High	84	188	204	96
1955	High	39	142	128	91
1956	High	69	103	143	118
1957	High	75	180	221	118
1958	High	49	111	79	51
1959	High	57	65	6	44
1960	High	74	64	38	71
1961	High	20	44	29	18
1962	High	61	84	25	54
1963	High	41	20	1	50
1964	High	5	−32	−8	33
1965	High	−6	−21	−2	53
1966	High	20	7	−2	107

(continued)

Table 2.1   *(Continued)*

Year	Price	+5 Years (%)	+10 Years (%)	+15 Years (%)	+20 Years (%)
1967	High	15	−22	−4	73
1968	High	−15	−28	7	83
1969	Above Average	−36	−13	26	167
1970	Above Average	−16	4	63	147
1971	Above Average	−10	−18	73	183
1972	High	−32	−17	51	157
1973	Low	−16	26	115	251
1974	Low	35	96	314	429
1975	Low	24	94	195	453
1976	Low	−8	93	215	457
1977	Low	23	123	279	739
1978	Low	49	155	316	987
1979	Low	45	206	292	1,123
1980	Low	57	138	346	813
1981	Low	111	245	508	805
1982	Low	81	208	582	?
1983	Below Average	71	179	630	?
1984	Below Average	111	170	742	?
1985	Above Average	52	185	483	?
1986	High	64	189	330	?
1987	High	70	276	?	?

for price-sensitive investors. The value-conscious investor does his buying precisely when no one else can stand the sight of stocks, like during the Great Depression, or the mid-1970s, when the stock market had lost half of its value. Nobody wanted to hear about stocks then. People hated stocks. That is when the astute Market Timer takes out his wallet and steps up to the table to buy.

It takes psychological fortitude to go against the crowd. By definition, stock prices will be highest when everyone is clamoring to buy them. By definition, stock prices will be lowest when the outlook for the market is dire. Moving with the herd is psychologically gratifying and gives us a feeling of security—even if the herd is rushing off a cliff. Relinquishing this safety blanket is the emotional price that must be paid for getting outsized returns by Market Timing. This emotional price is real, as you may see the next time a bubble hits and you ogle a new Lexus in the driveway of your idiot day-trading neighbor. A new bubble is unlikely in our lifetimes, but it could happen. If it does, remember these graphs and tables.

Unlike other stock market anomalies, which disappear the moment they are pointed out, buying low promises to endure. This is because the extra returns it delivers do not come free. Rather, they are a payment for assuming the psychological burden of buying stocks when everyone says the sky is falling, and demurring when Wall Street is having a feeding frenzy.

LUMP SUM INVESTING BASED ON MARKET PRICE ALONE

Consider another situation: the case of two lucky individuals, each with $50,000 to invest in the stock market at some point during the past century. One of them, taking Wall Street's Panglossian advice, invests his $50,000 paying no heed to the market's price. The other, a daring and resourceful Market Timer, invests his swag only at the end of a year when the market sells below its long-term price. Who would have invested more wisely, on average?

We measured the returns for each year-end rolling 20-year period from 1901 to 1981 (since the later 20-year returns are not in yet), and averaged the results both types of investors would have achieved. The *whenever* investor gets the average of all 20-year returns, while the Market Timer enjoys the 20-year average returns from only those years when the S&P 500 was selling below its long-term moving average.

The lump sum investor who bought stocks whenever would have patiently watched his $50,000 investment grow to $218,500 on average over the subsequent 20 years, an annualized return of 7.7 percent. The Market Timer who bought stocks on the cheap would have watched his $50,000 investment grow to $313,500 on average over the same period. This would have proved an annualized return of 9.6 percent, putting the Market Timer $95,000 to the good—some 25 percent better.

Of course, in practice, the Non-Market Timing lump sum investor does not invest in an "average" year. He invests in a *particular* year—one that is either above or below the long-term moving average. If the price that year is below the average, he gets the same results as the Market Timer. But if he invests in a year when the price is above the moving average, his results will be significantly worse than the average mentioned above. They will be more like the results shown in Figure 2.4.

To look at it another way, the buy-whenever guy's worst-case scenario total real return in the last century was to discover that his $50,000 kitty had grown to only $59,000. The worst news the Market Timer would have found over any subsequent 20-year stretch was that his investment had grown to $83,500. What does this tell us? Simply this: Buying low is not only a recipe for outsized returns on the upside, it is an excellent defense against future bear markets. Price-based Market Timing is a sensible way to decide when to jump into the stock market.

DOLLAR COST AVERAGING USING MARKET PRICE ALONE

Dollar cost averaging is an investment strategy endorsed by Wall Street for all the "little people" who do not have large sums of money to invest at one time, but who might be able to accommodate a regular program of smaller contributions to an investment account—typically monthly or yearly. Often these are automatic fixed withdrawals from a paycheck into a retirement plan or from a checking account into a mutual fund. The dollar cost averager is effectively a Market Timer who believes that every month or every year is equally a good time to invest. Wall Street is quick to point out that when the market goes down, this is really good news because your fixed dollars buy even more shares at these times. Of course, when the market goes up, your fixed dollars buy fewer shares. This part is not emphasized. The assumption seems to be, as long as the market is up, who cares how many shares you are getting for your dollar? It is presented as a win-win situation for investors. But is it? In fact, picking and choosing when to invest instead of simply averaging in every year has yielded decisively better results.

Imagine that at the end of 1901, two investors resolved to buy into the stock market at the end of each year throughout the new century. One, heeding Wall Street's siren song, decides to dollar cost average into the market at the end of every year, rain or shine. The second, a judicious and circumspect Market Timer, vows only to buy the S&P 500 at the end of each year when its price is below that of the 15-year trend line. Their final fate is graphed in Figure 2.6.

The dollar cost average guy has achieved a whopping 951 percent total real return on his investment. His $100,000 (year 2001 dollars) has grown to be $1,051,008. No doubt about it, the twentieth century has been a terrific time to buy stocks, and his prescience has been abundantly rewarded. He has done well.

However, look at the Market Timer. Since he knows in advance that he is going to be buying only about half of the time, he doubles up on his investments when stocks are cheap and keeps his money in the bank when they are not. This way he puts in $2,000 every time he thinks stocks are worth buying, while his dollar cost averaging pal ponies up $1,000 every year no matter what.

The Market Timer, however, attained a 1,433 percent return on his kitty. The Market Timer only found 40 years during the century when stocks were priced to his liking, so his initial outlay

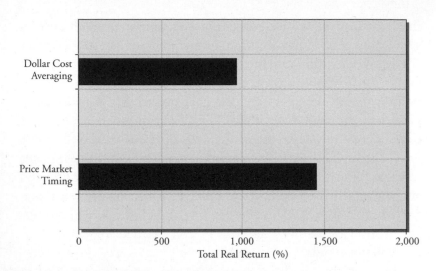

**Figure 2.6   Dollar Cost Averaging versus
Price-Based Market Timing, 1902–2001**

was $80,000. His holdings are now priced at $1,226,213—a 1,443 percent return. This is a 51 percent better return than the dollar cost averager achieved (and this does not even include his cash position). The large difference is entirely due to Market Timing.

1977–2001

Let us move the analysis closer to our own time. Imagine that both of our investor friends opened 401(k) plans in 1977 with the option of making monthly contributions.

This time, the dollar cost averager sinks $100 of his hard-earned pay in the S&P 500 at the end of every month no matter what the price of the stock market. The Market Timer plows in $200 each time, but only buys when the price is below the long-term trend line, as shown in Figure 2.7.

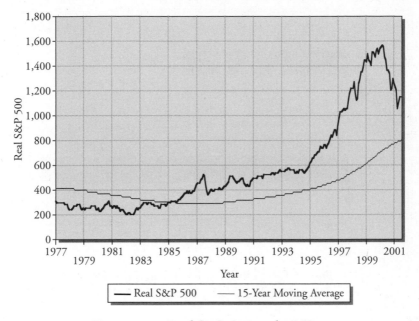

Figure 2.7   Real S&P 500 and 15-Year Moving Average, 1977–2002

This isn't quantum mechanics. The Market Timer buys stocks through June of 1985. Then the market price line crosses the 15-year moving average heading up, and stocks become too expensive for his Spartan taste. So for the rest of the period, he sits on the sidelines, reinvesting his dividends, but otherwise quiescent.

By the end of 2001, the dollar cost averager has pumped $30,000 of his own money into the market in hundred-dollar dollops, and seen it grow to $75,059 over that same period—a gain of 150 percent. The Market Timer only found occasion to invest $20,400 of his dollars over the same period. But his account now holds $78,180—a gain of 283 percent, fully 89 percent better for the funds invested than his buying-all-the-time friend. Their relative fortunes are shown in Figure 2.8.

Using a simple comparison of where the market is priced today next to its long-term price level, the Market Timer achieves

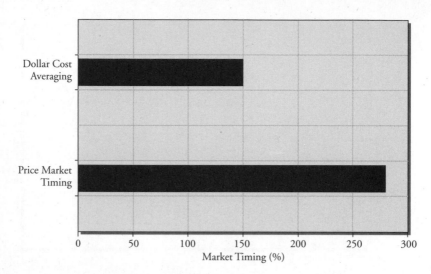

Figure 2.8 Dollar Cost Averaging versus Price-Based Market Timing, 1977–2001

superior returns by buying low. It seems too simple to be true, but so far it has been.

Did we mention that the Market Timer has been sitting on some cash for the past 15 years waiting for the price of the stock market to strike his fancy again? If he put it into bonds during this interlude, it is now worth an extra $17,271. This brings his grand total to $95,451, compared to his pal's $75,059. Even if the Market Timer sunk his cash into boring, completely riskless T-bills, he now has an extra $11,427 of "walking around" money, for a total pot of $89,607. Could it be that there is something to Market Timing after all?

Having observed how the stock market behaves in terms of price, let us look at some other price-related measures that tell us something about stock market valuation. The first of these is the engine that makes the whole thing run: corporate earnings. We now turn to a popular stock market metric to see whether it can help us time the market: the *price/earnings ratio.*

Chapter Three

The Price/Earnings Ratio

The most fundamental metric besides raw price that you can apply to a stock is the *price/earnings ratio.* Sometimes referred to as the *p/e* or the *multiple,* this is the price of the stock divided by the company's earnings per share. When you purchase a share of stock, you get more than a fancy certificate suitable for framing: You actually own a small piece of a company, and to that extent, you enjoy the company's profits. The stock's price/earnings ratio tells how much it costs to dip into this income stream.

The meaning of price by itself is limited without knowing the earnings. If you were going to buy an apartment building, it would be impossible to come up with a rational price to pay for it unless you knew what the stream of rental income was. It could be ocean-front property in sunny Santa Monica, California—but if the apartment building was rent-controlled by the city (as some are, in fact), it would command a low price, because an owner cannot recoup enough in rentals to cover more than a small mortgage. One of your authors briefly lived in a rundown apartment building called "Montezuma Hall" during college. Next to a campus with a captive student population, this hovel was nevertheless a cash cow for the owners and could have sold for a fortune, given the inelastic demand for rentals there and the soaring prices they could claim. Yet, if you were to drive by these two very different properties, you would get a completely misleading impression as to their real worth. Price depends on earnings.

As Fidelity's Peter Lynch succinctly puts it, "Ultimately, corporate earnings drive the market. It's that simple." When the price of a stock or the entire market disconnects from its underlying earnings, something has to give. This can happen for a time, but ultimately they stay in a very rough equilibrium. Looking at a historical graph of stock market prices and earnings was what allowed Yale University economist Robert Shiller to foretell the bursting of the 1990s stock market bubble in his salutary book, *Irrational Exuberance.*

The *price* is unambiguous enough for a publicly traded company: It is what the stock currently sells for on the open market. A company's *earnings* are its profits after taxes: all the money that is available to be distributed to shareholders in the form of dividends, or reinvested in the company in pursuit of future growth. A company that sells for a price/earnings multiple of 10 gave you a dollar in earnings last year for your 10 dollars' worth of stock. A company that sells for a price/earnings ratio of 30 charges you 30 dollars for that same dollar in earnings.

Why would anyone pay a price/earnings multiple of 30 when he could find a stock with a price/earnings multiple of 10? Because the stock with the higher price/earnings multiple presumably has a higher growth rate. That is, investors are hoping to get in early on a company that will one day reward them with a torrent of dividends and earnings. Even if these people sell their shares before these goodies materialize, they will seek to sell them at a premium to someone who in turn plans to realize the supersized dividends already factored into the price today. These investors are taking a risk *now* in the hope of securing a big return *later*. Unfortunately, for every high price/earnings multiple stock that becomes the next Intel, others will go out of business. If you have had trouble getting your pizza from Kozmo.com or your groceries delivered by HomeGrocer.com lately, it is because these companies are now bankrupt.

In his investment classic *The Intelligent Investor,* Benjamin Graham recommended using the price/earnings ratio as a tool to screen stocks. But, instead of looking for turbocharged growth stocks, his goal was to discover beaten down, unloved companies that were underpriced by investors and hence had the best capacity for price appreciation. With the advent of the Internet and the ability of anyone to instantly sift through thousands of stocks with the push of a button, these undervalued gems have become harder to find than in Graham's day. Graham felt that growth stocks with high price/earnings multiples generally made poor investments.

Investors love a good story, and these (new technology, often) companies are the ones people get the most excited about. Because their prices race ahead at a high multiple of their earnings, these companies are thrilling for speculators to own when they are on their way up. But when earnings disappoint, their prices can plummet spectacularly. Shares of the red-hot Internet company incubator CMGI rocketed to over one thousand dollars in 1999. This company had no earnings and therefore a price/earnings multiple of infinity. If you liked the company at a thousand dollars a share, you'll like it even better today. It trades for thirty-five cents a share as of this writing.

Graham understood all of this, and so recommended that investors avoid any stock with a price/earnings ratio over 20. The most successful long-term investors have been those like Warren Buffett who follow this *value* orientation. Although some high-flying growth stocks as well as funky, downtrodden value companies will inevitably fail, the value-oriented investor pays a lower price for his mistakes.

There is empirical evidence to support Graham's belief in stocks with low price/earnings ratios:

- James O'Shaughnessy discovered that between 1951 and 1994, buying the 50 stocks in the S&P 500 with the lowest price/earnings ratios at the beginning of each year beat the market as a whole 88 percent of the time. The compound annual return of the low price/earnings stocks was 13.47 percent versus 11.41 percent for the S&P 500 over this period—some 18 percent better.
- Writing in the *Journal of Finance* in 1977, Sanjoy Basu looked at the stocks on the New York Stock Exchange each year from 1957 to 1971, ranking them into five groups, from those having the lowest to those having the highest price/earnings ratios. During the year that followed, the group with the highest price/earnings ratio

had an annual return of 9.3 percent, while the group with the lowest price/earnings ratio returned 16.3 percent with no added risk.

- Examining the period from 1967 to 1984, Roger Ibbotson divided the stocks of the New York Stock Exchange into deciles according to their price/earnings ratios. He found that those with the highest price/earnings ratios had an annual compound return of 5.6 percent over this 18-year period, while those selling at the lowest price/earnings ratio returned 14.1 percent annually: an improvement of 152 percent.

- Lakonishok, Vishny, and Shleifer divided the stocks on the New York and American Stock Exchanges into deciles by their price/earnings ratios from 1968 to 1990, and followed them for five years. The decile that sold at the highest price/earnings ratio had an average annual return of 11.4 percent in the five years following, while the decile with the lowest price/earnings ratio achieved an average annual return of 19 percent. (Reader please note: There are periods of relatively high return no matter how you choose, just as there are periods of relatively low return no matter how you choose.)

- Similar benefits to investing at low price/earnings ratios have been observed in stocks in England, Germany, France, Switzerland, and Japan. Surveying the international evidence, Dimson, Marsh, and Staunton estimate the overall value stock outperformance at .26 percent per month.

Why do low price/earnings stocks tend to rise in price more than high price/earnings stocks? The answer lies in the statistical concept of *regression to the mean*. This is a fancy way of saying that extreme scores tend to be followed by ones that are more usual. It explains why the price/earnings ratio (and other measures of value we will discuss) can be used to time the market.

A baseball slugger who is batting .333 for the season got three hits at three at-bats yesterday, batting 1000 for the day. Does this mean he's likely to bat 1000 today? No, his batting average is likely to regress to its very fine mean of around .333.

Today, this same slugger is struck out all three times he steps up to the plate, batting .000. Does this mean he should be fired because he's going to bat .000 from now on? No, his batting average is likely to regress to its mean, around .333.

Regression to the mean is the stretchy rubber band that powers most of the market timing measures in this book. Whenever a number strays too far out of line with our ordinary experience, the rubber band pulls it back—perhaps not all at once, perhaps not today, but eventually.

Extreme scores are more prone to contain some measure of error. There tends to be more "noise" in the system at the outside edges. If the person next to you on the freeway is driving a Rolls Royce, does this make it easier to guess his income? Well, yes and no. Possibly, he is a car buff or a status-seeking upper middle-class yuppie putting on airs, but probably he is a millionaire. However, he could be worth $10 million, $50 million, $100 million, or more. The range of answers is all over the map, but only one of them is correct. By the way, if you assume that the guy in the slow lane driving the 10-year-old pickup truck is poor, you haven't read Stanley and Danko's *The Millionaire Next Door* or you have never lived in the Midwest.

As stock prices and earnings reports from the companies they represent are retested day after day and year after year in the crucible of the market, these errors at the margin in terms of price/earnings are likely to be corrected over time and replaced with information that is more accurate. As this happens, the system reverts to equilibrium. The rubber band snaps back.

Would buying the stock market as a whole when its price/earnings ratio is low lead to superior returns in the years that followed, just as it did when buying individual stocks? What if we treated the 500 companies of the S&P Index as if they were a single stock with a single price/earnings ratio? If we bought the stock when its price/earnings ratio was low, would regression to the mean pull its price back up? If so, this means we could use the price/earnings ratio to time the entire market.

Over the past hundred years, the price/earnings of the S&P 500 has averaged around 16, and has generally ranged somewhere between 5 and 30. To see the century at a glance, the real (i.e., in-flation-adjusted) S&P 500 is shown in Figure 3.1. In Figure 3.2, the price/earnings ratio of the S&P 500 (the thick line) is graphed alongside its own 15-year moving average (the thin line).

In 1932, the price/earnings ratio skyrocketed to 130—too high to even fit on the chart. Although the price of stocks had been battered by the Depression, corporate earnings collapsed even further. Because the fall in the denominator (earnings) was greater than the fall in price, it caused the ratio to temporarily skyrocket. This was, we hope, a statistic unlikely to be repeated any time soon, and not to be considered except in prayers.

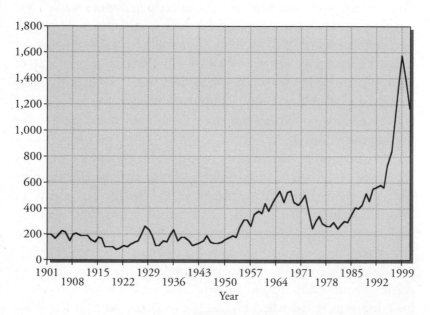

Figure 3.1   The Real S&P 500

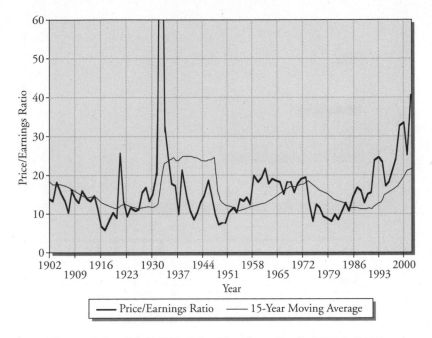

Figure 3.2   S&P 500 Price/Earnings Ratio, 1902–2001

To begin, we classified each year of the century according to where the price/earnings ratio stood in relation to its moving average. If it were above, we assumed stocks were expensive and we were buying high. If below, we assumed stocks were cheap and we were buying low. We measured the total returns that sprang from these cheap or expensive years over various periods of time. The results are shown in Figure 3.3. The result: Once we got past five years, buying the market when the price/earnings ratio is low beats the alternative. Not only were earnings important, we could use them to time the stock market.

Next, we wanted to find out whether it mattered how high or low the price/earnings ratio was at the time of stock purchase. Presumably, the farther the rubber band is stretched, the more it should snap back into position. We sorted the years of the century into quartiles, according to how high or low the price/earnings ratio was at the end of each year compared to its moving average.

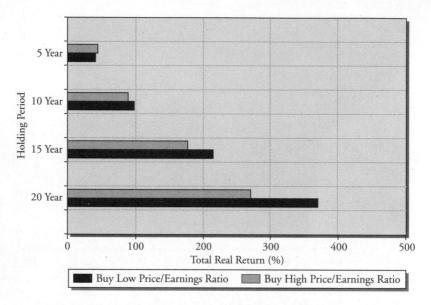

Figure 3.3   Price/Earnings Timed Investing, 1902–2001

The years with the highest 25 percent of price/earnings ratios went into the *High* stack, the next 25 percent went into the *Above Average* stack, the next highest went into the *Below Average* stack, and the lowest 25 percent of scores went into the *Low* stack. We then computed what the total 20-year returns were for having invested in each of these years, and averaged them for each quartile. The results are shown in Figure 3.4. Note the advantage that accrues to the investor who buys when price/earnings ratios are at their lowest. The High quartile was the worst time to buy in spite of benefiting from the anomalous jump in the price/earnings ratio in 1932.

Table 3.1 on pages 40 to 42 profiles each year of the century according to these price/earnings quartiles, and tracks the returns that followed from buying into the market that year. The results are impressive. Buying low helps to achieve superior returns.

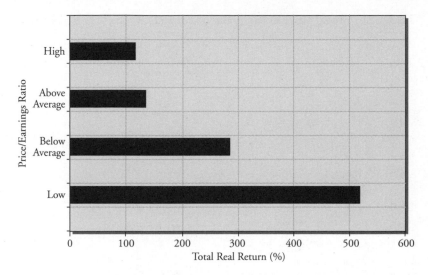

Figure 3.4 **Twenty-Year Average Total Real Return by P/E Ratio Quartile When Purchased, 1902–2001**

LUMP SUM INVESTING USING THE P/E RATIO

Again, consider the case of two fortunate individuals who have come into a lump sum of money. If they call their stockbrokers, the advice they would receive is predictable. Just as car salesmen often recommend that today is a good day to buy a car and real-tors are prone to believe that today is a good day to buy a house, so too with the financial securities industry. A stockbroker would confidently inform them that since everyone knows that you can-not time the market, the money should be invested *tout de suite.* At the limit, it should be parceled into the market over the course of one year: otherwise, the investor would be guilty of Market Timing. Reassurances will be given that even if the market col-lapses, any short-term gyrations will be more than repaid by pa-tiently keeping the money in the market over the long haul.

The first investor takes this "What—me worry?" approach and invests his $50,000 at once. The second, a crackerjack Market

Table 3.1   Total Real Returns Based on P/E Ratio When Invested

Year	P/E Ratio	+5 Years (%)	+10 Years (%)	+15 Years (%)	+20 Years (%)
1902	Low	−11	45	0	43
1903	Low	51	51	22	69
1904	Below Average	32	11	−2	64
1905	Low	4	27	−33	75
1906	Low	5	20	−16	97
1907	Low	64	12	61	305
1908	Below Average	0	−19	12	310
1909	Low	−16	−26	24	229
1910	Low	22	−36	68	186
1911	Above Average	14	−21	87	72
1912	Below Average	−31	−2	148	67
1913	Low	−19	12	311	186
1914	Above Average	−12	48	291	189
1915	Low	−47	38	135	209
1916	Low	−30	64	51	318
1917	Low	43	261	143	315
1918	Low	38	409	254	439
1919	Low	67	342	227	409
1920	Low	163	346	488	472
1921	HIGH	135	116	498	257
1922	Above Average	152	69	189	204
1923	Below Average	268	156	290	269
1924	Below Average	165	96	205	242
1925	Below Average	70	124	118	266
1926	Below Average	−8	154	52	147
1927	HIGH	−33	15	21	72
1928	HIGH	−30	6	0	19
1929	Above Average	−26	15	29	58
1930	HIGH	32	28	115	143
1931	HIGH	177	65	168	355
1932	HIGH	71	80	155	426
1933	Above Average	52	44	71	240
1934	Above Average	56	75	114	443

Table 3.1 *(Continued)*

Year	P/E Ratio	+5 Years (%)	+10 Years (%)	+15 Years (%)	+20 Years (%)
1935	Below Average	−3	64	84	399
1936	Below Average	−40	−3	65	297
1937	Low	5	49	208	450
1938	Below Average	−5	12	124	473
1939	Low	12	37	248	540
1940	Low	68	89	413	613
1941	Low	63	176	565	1,022
1942	Low	42	193	422	812
1943	Low	19	136	505	804
1944	Low	22	210	470	793
1945	Low	13	205	324	639
1946	Low	70	309	590	729
1947	Low	107	268	544	933
1948	Low	99	410	662	974
1949	Low	154	367	630	670
1950	Low	171	277	556	518
1951	Below Average	141	306	388	485
1952	Below Average	78	212	400	473
1953	Below Average	156	283	440	358
1954	Above Average	84	188	204	96
1955	Above Average	39	142	128	91
1956	Above Average	69	103	143	118
1957	Above Average	75	180	221	118
1958	High	49	111	79	51
1959	High	57	65	6	44
1960	High	74	64	38	71
1961	High	20	44	29	18
1962	High	61	84	25	54
1963	High	41	20	1	50
1964	High	5	−32	−8	33
1965	Above Average	−6	−21	−2	53
1966	Below Average	20	7	−2	107
1967	Above Average	15	−22	−4	73

(continued)

Table 3.1 *(Continued)*

Year	P/E Ratio	+5 Years (%)	+10 Years (%)	+15 Years (%)	+20 Years (%)
1968	Above Average	−15	−28	7	83
1969	Below Average	−36	−13	26	167
1970	Above Average	−16	4	63	147
1971	Above Average	−10	−18	73	183
1972	Above Average	−32	−17	51	157
1973	Low	−16	26	115	251
1974	Low	35	96	314	429
1975	Low	24	94	195	453
1976	Low	−8	93	215	457
1977	Low	23	123	279	739
1978	Low	49	155	316	987
1979	Low	45	206	292	1,123
1980	Low	57	138	346	813
1981	Low	111	245	508	805
1982	Low	81	208	582	?
1983	Above Average	71	179	630	?
1984	Low	111	170	742	?
1985	High	52	185	483	?
1986	High	64	189	330	?
1987	High	70	276	?	?
1988	Above Average	63	326	?	?
1989	High	28	299	?	?
1990	High	88	284	?	?
1991	High	77	163	?	?
1992	High	121	?	?	?
1993	High	161	?	?	?
1994	Above Average	212	?	?	?
1995	Above Average	105	?	?	?
1996	High	49	?	?	?
1997	High	?	?	?	?
1998	High	?	?	?	?
1999	High	?	?	?	?
2000	High	?	?	?	?
2001	High	?	?	?	?

Timer, looks askance at the broker's glib response and makes a mental note only to invest his $50,000 in a year when the price/earnings ratio is below its 15-year moving average.

We took the starting point of the Non-Market Timer as any of the last 100 years up to 1981, or more properly, all of them. The Market Timer's starting points were only those years when the price/earnings ratio was below its 15-year moving average.

We examined the total real returns for each succeeding and overlapping 20-year period, starting in 1902 and ending in 1981 (we do not know the 20-year returns thereafter). We averaged the returns coming from years when the price/earnings ratio was low—when our Market Timer would have been buying—and compared these to the average of all years (both the high and the low price/earnings years) when our Non-Market Timer might have sunk his or her treasure into the market.

By trusting to a low price/earnings ratio rather than to luck, the Market Timer secured a superior return for his fortune: he does 34 percent better on average over each 20-year span. This means he now has $276,000 on average in stock assets versus his friend's $218,500. That phone call to his broker turned out to be expensive for the Non-Market Timer. The size of the price/earnings ratio at the time of buying into the market makes an enormous difference to investment performance.

DOLLAR COST AVERAGING

Imagine that in 1901, two forward-looking individuals resolved to become investors in the coming century. One, a dollar cost averager, buys into the market every year, adding to his position no matter how the market is faring. The second, a Market Timer, only buys the S&P 500 when its price/earnings multiple rests below its own 15-year moving average.

The Market Timer would have bought stocks pretty much through the mid-1920s, then again in the mid-1930s through the mid-1950s, and last in the 1970s and early 1980s. He would not have bought stocks at the end of the roaring 1920s. He would have passed on the electronics boom of the 1960s and the "nifty fifty" stocks of the early 1970s, and sidestepped entirely the biotech bonanza of the 1980s and the Internet bubble of the 1990s. This would have made him the most boring person at any cocktail party of the century.

What it will not have made him is poor. Figure 3.5 shows the Market Timer's total return, compared with the person who dollar cost averaged into the market over the same period.

Buying low has earned the Market Timer a total return (including reinvested dividends) of 1,294 percent versus 951 percent for dollar cost averaging—a 36 percent improvement in performance for the Market Timer. Even so, the Market Timer did far from perfectly. As we mentioned before, in 1932 the price/earnings ratio of the S&P 500 soared to 130—its highest point ever—due to the near-total disappearance of earnings. In fact, stocks were extraordinarily cheap that year. The price/earnings ratio gave

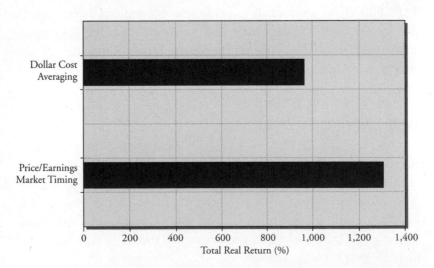

**Figure 3.5   Dollar Cost Averaging versus
Market Timing, 1902–2001**

the wrong signal to the Market Timer, although green lights for buying stocks were flashing from other metrics, including the simple "price" standard we explored in the previous chapter. Even so, the outperformance the Market Timer achieved using only the price/earnings ratio as his guide more than made up for this mistake. (People looking for perfection would be well advised to avoid the stock market altogether.)

Since the Market Timer plans to buy only when the price/earnings ratio is below its average, he knows in advance that he will be buying roughly half the time. This means he can double his investments compared to the person who consistently dollar cost averages into the market year after year. Starting at the end of 1902, had he invested $2000 (in year 2001 dollars) at the end of every year when the price/earnings ratio sank below its 15-year moving average, his $106,000 dollar investment would have swelled to $1,487,055 by the end of 2001, for a total real return of 1,294 percent. The dollar cost averager who put in $1,000 every year, come what may, would have seen his investment of $100,000 grow to $1,051,080, a total real return of 951 percent. The dollar cost averager has nothing to reproach himself about. Still, given the choice, most people would take the Market Timer's extra $435,975. It buys a lot of plastic flamingoes to put around the trailer court.

1977–2001

Given that there is a broad trend favoring stocks with low price/earnings multiples, and that this wisdom extends to buying the market as a whole when it is cheaply priced by this measure, we are not surprised to learn that this also holds true for the monthly investor over the past 25 years.

Consider the fate of two investors. The dollar cost averager invests in the stock market at the end of every month from 1977–2001, buying at the market price. The Market Timer only imbibes during those months when the price/earnings ratio of the market is below the 15-year moving average. Figure 3.6 shows the inflation-adjusted S&P 500 and Figure 3.7 shows the monthly price/earnings ratio and 15-year moving average over the same period.

Note how the investor seeking the low price/earnings multiple would have been buying stocks all during the 1970s, when everyone else was buying gold. Then, except for partaking in 1995, he would have sat on his hands during most of the bull market of the 1980s and 1990s, watching his portfolio grow, but keeping any new money in the bank. This is exactly the opposite of what he would have been tempted to do had he been watching CNBC. His restraint would have been rewarded, as shown in Figure 3.8 on page 48.

The dollar cost averager who put $100 into the market every month no matter what would have seen his $30,000 stake grow to $75,059, for a total real return of 150 percent. The Market

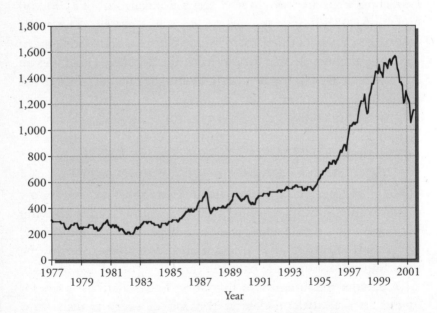

Figure 3.6   Real S&P 500, 1977–2001

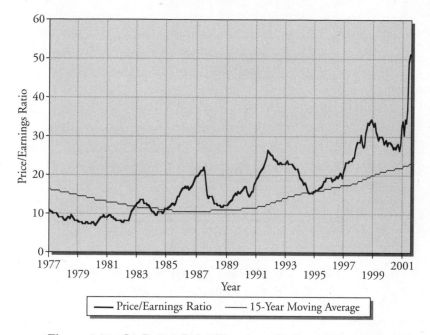

Figure 3.7   S&P 500 Price/Earnings Ratio, 1977–2001

Timer who invested $200 at the end of every month when the current price/earnings ratio was below its long-term average would have seen his $18,400 investment (2001 dollars) grow to $71,090, for a total real return of 286 percent—some 91 percent better than the dollar cost averager, but with a smaller stock portfolio to show for it. However, he also has $14,036 of principal + interest sitting in T-bills, awaiting the next market opportunity. The Market Timer's grand total is $85,126 overall for a total real return of 183 percent—handily beating the dollar cost averager's 150 percent.

Contrary to the "stocks for all seasons" doctrine promoted by the financial services industry, the Market Timer, armed with nothing more than the price/earnings ratio of the S&P 500, does better buying low. However, there is a worm in our investment Eden. Our data benefits unfairly from *look-ahead bias.* This is because we typically do not learn the S&P's earnings until the

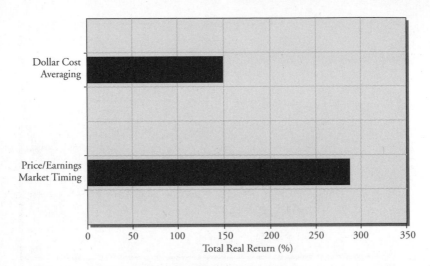

**Figure 3.8   Dollar Cost Averaging versus
P/E Market Timing, 1977–2001**

quarter *after* they were gleaned. Is the theoretical benefit on the side of the Market Timer capturable in the real world, where earnings data are released a quarter late?

We can simulate a real-world stock purchaser by backshifting the data in the monthly 1977–2001 database. Under this new real-world scenario, while the dollar cost averager continues to buy every month as before, the Market Timer is now blinded by only having access to the earnings data from the previous quarter, while having to buy stock at the price today. Thus, he buys a quarter late. The results are shown in Figure 3.9.

Sadly, the real world return over this period drops from the pure theoretical model. From 286 percent to 274 percent. Surely this is a disappointment that an investor can bear. The power of the price/earnings ratio to describe the stock market's valuation overwhelms the quarterly time lag problem in earnings reports.

Now, you might ask, isn't this price/earnings ratio a slippery concept?

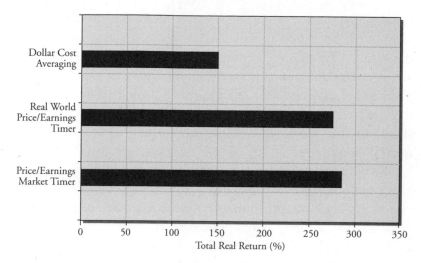

**Figure 3.9   Dollar Cost Averaging versus "Real World"
P/E Timing, 1977–2001**

Yes. Since it passes through the corporate finance department, it is subject to all manner of manipulation en route to public consumption. Not the price, which is a matter of public record, but the earnings. Chief financial officers (CFOs) are always trying to exclude items from the balance sheet that might negatively impact a firm's earnings (and hence its stock price). There are "as reported" earnings, "operating" earnings, and "pro forma" earnings, each admitting progressively freer definition. Still worse are "forward-looking earnings" (AKA "next year's earnings"), which truly require a crystal ball. The historical price/earnings ratios of the S&P 500 used herein are of the "as reported" trailing one-year variety. Accept no substitute. Only "as reported" earnings allow you to make valid historical comparisons. As treacherous as earnings reports can be, they are still of considerable value. If they become total fictions, however, they will lose their utility for investors of almost any kind.

If history is any guide (and we can think of no other), the long-term investor armed with the S&P 500's price/earnings ratio can time the market to his considerable profit. The price/earnings ratio of the S&P 500 is published in *Barron's* every Saturday, in the "Market Laboratory" section. As an immediate point of comparison, consider that this ratio has averaged around 16 for the past century. Although the price/earnings ratio is of no use to the day trader or near-term speculator, the conservative investor should be able to employ it to enhance his returns over his investment lifetime.

Recently, the shenanigans of the CFOs and auditors have given the whole subject of corporate earnings a black eye. Investors are beginning to pine once more for that portion of the earnings that actually is distributed to them, the *dividend*. We now turn to the subject of the dividend yield, to see whether it can be exploited to time the stock market.

Chapter Four

Dividend Yields and
Market Timing

What does a company do with its earnings?

First of all, they can be reinvested in the company's operations to maintain or expand the business.

Alternatively, the company can use them to buy back its own shares from the market, possibly thereby boosting its stock price.

When the stock market took off during the 1990s, many corporations inadvertently found themselves running their pension plans as profit centers, and so started to invest some of their profits back into the stock market as another way to boost revenues. In some cases, these stock market returns (temporarily) eclipsed the profits from their core businesses.

Finally, as a last resort, companies can elect to actually distribute some of their earnings directly to their owners, the shareholders. That is when companies issue dividends. For centuries, this was the major use of earnings. But in recent years, dividends as a percentage of earnings have fallen dramatically (although total dividend payments have risen sharply).

Today companies often like to avoid paying dividends. CEOs paternalistically believe that they can dream up better uses for the money to better their lowly shareholders than the shareholders can for themselves. Plus, as of this writing, dividend checks are fully taxable as ordinary income to stockholders, even after already having been taxed as corporate profits. Personal income taxes are postponed on undistributed earnings, and might be transmuted into capital gains that will be taxed at a probable lower rate in the future. In this respect, dividends have become a casualty of being double-taxed by the government.

There are reasons to like dividends, though. If a company cuts you a dividend check, and the check clears at your bank, it is likely that the company actually had the earnings in the first place. They were not just numbers picked from the air by crooked management, foisted on a hack board of directors, and then sold to gullible Wall Street analysts while the Securities and Exchange Commission (SEC) and the financial press slumbered. The difference between dividends and earnings is the difference between having cash in your bank account versus holding a paper IOU signed by the chief executive. As old-fashioned and tax-disadvantaged as dividends may be, they have the virtue of being real.

If you add up all the dividends paid by the 500 big companies in the Standard & Poor's (S&P) composite index, and divide this sum by the price of all their shares, you get the S&P 500's *dividend yield.* This is the percentage of the price of the companies you get back each year in consideration for being an owner. The yield has varied widely over the century. In 1940, stocks gave you roughly 8 percent back in dividends. In 2002, the dividend yield was only about 1.4 percent.

There are two ways of looking at this phenomenon. One way would be to focus on the numerator, the dividends, and pronounce that dividends have fallen out of favor, which surely they have. This view is popular on Wall Street. Another would be to look at the denominator, the price of the S&P 500, and conclude that stocks are presently overpriced. This latter argument also seems to have merit. Probably both are true. In any event, the dividend yield is another conventional indicator of stock market valuation. When dividends are high, it is thought that stocks are cheap. When dividends are low, stocks are expensive.

Figure 4.1 plots the real S&P 500 over the past 100 years alongside the dividend yield stocks have paid over this same period. You can see that there is a rough negative correlation between the two: when one is up, more often than not, the other is down. Dividend yields have averaged around 4 percent over the last century, and tended to return to this mean when they strayed from it. This regression to the mean is what we exploit to use the dividend yield to time the market.

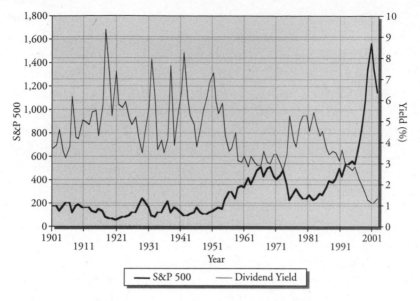

Figure 4.1   S&P 500 versus Dividend Yield

We didn't pull this out of a hat. In 1930, the great Yale economist Irving Fisher famously defined the value of an investment as the sum of all its future dividends, discounted back to their present value. In 1962, Myron Gordon expanded Fisher's insight into a formula that estimates the stock market's current value from its dividend rate, the historical growth of that dividend rate, and the rate at which these dividends are discounted back to the present. Dividends and stock prices are joined at the hip:

- Vanguard's John Bogle looked at the period from 1935 to 1992 and observed that when the dividend yield was under 3.5 percent, the odds of having a total annual return of over 10 percent during the next decade were 1 in 16. When the dividend yield was over 4.6 percent, the odds of getting a 10 percent total annual return rose to 19 chances out of 27.

- Michael Keppler, writing in the *Journal of Portfolio Management* in 1991, looked at the relationship between dividend yields and stock market performance in 17 countries around the world (including the United States). Every three months over the period from 1969 to 1989, he sorted the stocks in the local markets into four quartiles, according to how high a dividend yield the stocks were offering. He then looked at the performance of these stocks over the following quarter. He discovered that the quartile with the highest yielding stocks rose at an annual rate of 18 percent on average, while the one containing the lowest yielding stocks rose only 6 percent.

- Mario Levis reported similar findings in the *Journal of Banking and Finance* for 1989. Levis ranked all the companies in the London Stock Exchange from 1955 to 1988 into deciles according to their dividend yields. The decile with the highest dividend yields returned 19.3 percent on average each following year; the decile with the lowest returned only 13.8 percent.

- Writing for the *Financial Analysts Journal,* Arnott and Asness found that between 1871 and 2001, corporate profits grew fastest in the decade following the highest dividend payouts, and was lowest in the years following the lowest dividend payouts.

How should we judge the generosity of the dividend yield for the stock market as a whole? The same way we judge the price of gas at the pump: by comparing what it is currently with what it has been historically. Figure 4.2 tracks the dividend yield of the S&P 500 Index against its own 15-year moving average. Our strategy will be to buy into the stock market when companies are paying us a lot of money to own their stock, so the current dividend yield is above its long-term average. That is when the thick

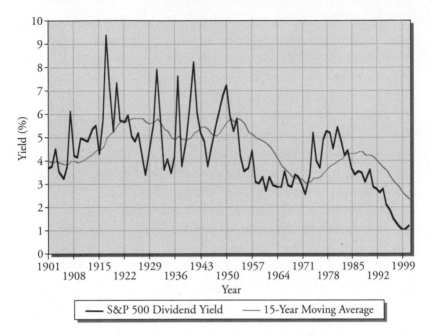

Figure 4.2   S&P Dividend Yield, 1901–2001

line is above the thin line in Figure 4.2. When companies are being stingy with their dividends, we will snub them and find other uses for our money. That is, we will buy when the dividend yield is historically high and avoid buying when it is low.

Does it make a difference whether we invest above or below the trend line? First, we assumed that an investor bought at the end of each of the years during the century when stocks were expensive (that is, when the dividend yield was below its long-term moving average). Then we calculated how his investment had performed if he sold it exactly 5, 10, 15, and 20 years later. For stocks bought at the end of 1901, we looked at the total real returns from selling at the end of 1906, 1911, 1916, and 1921. For stocks bought in 1902, we computed their total real returns as of 1907, 1912, 1917, and 1922, and so on. Then we averaged all these returns by their holding period: all the 5-year returns, all the 10-year returns, all the 15-year returns, and all the 20-year returns.

We did the same for an investor who bought when the dividend yield of the S&P 500 was above its long-term average and stocks looked cheap. We measured his returns for each subsequent 5-, 10-, 15-, and 20-year period, and averaged all of these total returns by their holding period.

Figure 4.3 shows that over the average 5-, 10-, 15-, and 20-year holding periods throughout the last century, investors were better served by buying the market when the dividend yield was high. Furthermore, the performance advantage of the Market Timer improved the longer his time in the market.

Did it matter how high or low the dividend yield was at the time of investment? We sorted the dividend yield offered at the end of each year over the century into quartiles, according to where it stood relative to its 15-year moving average. The top 25 percent dividend yields (that is, those highest above the moving average) we marked "High." The second group that was above the

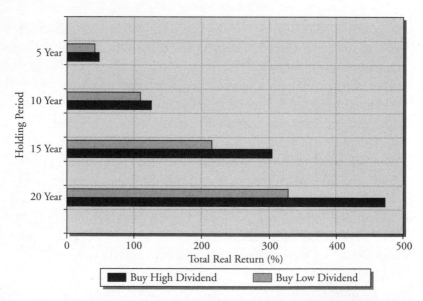

Figure 4.3   Dividend-Timed Investing, 1902–2001

moving average we labeled "Above Average," the group just below the moving average we labeled "Below Average," and the years with the lowest 25 percent of dividend yields we labeled "Low." Then we examined what the total real returns were for the years in each of these quartiles 20 years later. The results are shown in Figure 4.4. The higher the dividend yield at the time of stock purchase, the better the returns; the lower the dividend yield at the time of stock purchase, the worse the ensuing returns.

Table 4.1 shows the past one hundred years, with a rating of where the dividend yield of the S&P 500 stood in relation to its 15-year moving average (sorted into the quartiles described above). It shows the range of returns that would have been obtained had you invested at the end of each year.

The story this table tells is the same one we heard before: The people who glean the best investment returns are the ones who go shopping when stocks are on sale. Buy into a bull market (the 1920s, the 1960s, the 1990s) and you will have a hard time

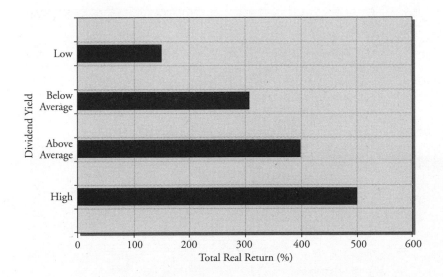

Figure 4.4   Twenty-Year Total Real Return by Dividend Yield Quartile When Purchased, 1902–2001

Table 4.1   Total Real Returns Based on Dividend Yield When Purchased

Year	Dividend Yield	+5 Years (%)	+10 Years (%)	+15 Years (%)	+20 Years (%)
1902	Below Average	−11	45	0	43
1903	High	51	51	22	69
1904	Low	32	11	−2	64
1905	Low	4	27	−33	75
1906	Below Average	5	20	−16	97
1907	High	64	12	61	305
1908	Above Average	0	−19	12	310
1909	Above Average	−16	−26	24	229
1910	High	22	−36	68	186
1911	High	14	−21	87	72
1912	High	−31	−2	148	67
1913	High	−19	12	311	186
1914	High	−12	48	291	189
1915	Below Average	−47	38	135	209
1916	High	−30	64	51	318
1917	High	43	261	143	315
1918	High	38	409	254	439
1919	Below Average	67	342	227	409
1920	High	163	346	488	472
1921	Above Average	135	116	498	257
1922	Below Average	152	69	189	204
1923	Above Average	268	156	290	269
1924	Low	165	96	205	242
1925	Low	70	124	118	266
1926	Low	−8	154	52	147
1927	Low	−33	15	21	72
1928	Low	−30	6	0	19
1929	Low	−26	15	29	58
1930	Below Average	32	28	115	143
1931	High	177	65	168	355
1932	Above Average	71	80	155	426
1933	Low	52	44	71	240
1934	Low	56	75	114	443

Table 4.1 *(Continued)*

Year	Dividend Yield	+5 Years (%)	+10 Years (%)	+15 Years (%)	+20 Years (%)
1935	Low	−3	64	84	399
1936	Low	−40	−3	65	297
1937	High	5	49	208	450
1938	Below Average	−5	12	124	473
1939	Above Average	12	37	248	540
1940	High	68	89	413	613
1941	High	63	176	565	1,022
1942	Above Average	42	193	422	812
1943	Below Average	19	136	505	804
1944	Below Average	22	210	470	793
1945	Low	13	205	324	639
1946	Below Average	70	309	590	729
1947	Above Average	107	268	544	933
1948	High	99	410	662	974
1949	High	154	367	630	670
1950	High	171	277	556	518
1951	Above Average	141	306	388	485
1952	Below Average	78	212	400	473
1953	Above Average	156	283	440	358
1954	Low	84	188	204	96
1955	Low	39	142	128	91
1956	Low	69	103	143	118
1957	Below Average	75	180	221	118
1958	Low	49	111	79	51
1959	Low	57	65	6	44
1960	Low	74	64	38	71
1961	Low	20	44	29	18
1962	Low	61	84	25	54
1963	Low	41	20	1	50
1964	Low	5	−32	−8	33
1965	Low	−6	−21	−2	53
1966	Below Average	20	7	−2	107
1967	Low	15	−22	−4	73
1968	Below Average	−15	−28	7	83

(continued)

Table 4.1   *(Continued)*

Year	Dividend Yield	+5 Years (%)	+10 Years (%)	+15 Years (%)	+20 Years (%)
1969	Above Average	−36	−13	26	167
1970	Above Average	−16	4	63	147
1971	Below Average	−10	−18	73	183
1972	Below Average	−32	−17	51	157
1973	Above Average	−16	26	115	251
1974	High	35	96	314	429
1975	High	24	94	195	453
1976	Above Average	−8	93	215	457
1977	High	23	123	279	739
1978	High	49	155	316	987
1979	High	45	206	292	1,123
1980	High	57	138	346	813
1981	High	111	245	508	805
1982	High	81	208	582	?
1983	Above Average	71	179	630	?
1984	Above Average	111	170	742	?
1985	Low	52	185	483	?
1986	Low	64	189	330	?
1987	Low	70	276	?	?
1988	Low	63	326	?	?
1989	Low	28	299	?	?
1990	Low	88	284	?	?
1991	Low	77	163	?	?
1992	Low	121	?	?	?
1993	Low	161	?	?	?
1994	Low	212	?	?	?
1995	Low	105	?	?	?
1996	Low	49	?	?	?
1997	Low	?	?	?	?
1998	Low	?	?	?	?
1999	Low	?	?	?	?
2000	Low	?	?	?	?
2001	Low	?	?	?	?

making money, because your cost basis is so high. Price relative to dividends matters greatly.

LUMP SUM INVESTING USING DIVIDEND YIELD

Suppose two investors each have a lump sum of $50,000 to invest at some point during the past century. One, a clever Market Timer, decides to buy when companies pay a dividend yield above its 15-year moving average. The other investor ignores this factor, and buys the S&P Index whenever it strikes his fancy.

We looked at every rolling 20-year period throughout the century to see how their lump sum investments would have performed, on average. For the buy-whenever investor, we looked at all 20-year real year-end returns and averaged these to get his result. For the Market Timer, we only took that subset of 20-year total returns following those years when the dividend yield was above its long-term trend line. We averaged these returns to get his outcome.

Twenty years later, the dividend-ignoring investor has patiently watched his $50,000 investment grow to $218,500, for a total return of 337 percent. The Market Timer who buys the rich dividend yield finds his $50,000 investment has grown to $283,500 over the same period. This represents a total return of 467 percent—some 39 percent better than his friend, an extra $65,000 of mint sauce. In the worst case (1961–1981), the person who bought into the market indifferent to the dividend yield would have seen his $50,000 turn to $59,000—hardly a wonderful total real return for 20 years. The person who waited for a big dividend would have watched his $50,000 grow to $83,500 in the worst instance (1912–1932). This is not a great total return, either, but human nature being what it is, perhaps he will take some consolation in knowing that at least he is $24,500 better off, almost 50 percent, than his Non-Market Timing chum.

DOLLAR COST AVERAGING

If our two investors did not have a lump sum to let the market digest, they might have tried feeding their money into the market in bite-sized portions throughout the century. One, a dollar cost averager, puts $1,000 (in 2001 dollars) into the market at the end of every year. The other, a winsome Market Timer, chooses to buy only when companies are paying a handsome dividend to attract investors and stocks are cheap. He buys at the end of those years when the dividend yield is above its 15-year moving average. Since he expects to be buying only about half the time, he doubles up to $2,000 when he buys and keeps his money earning interest in the bank when he is on the sidelines. The total returns are compared in Figure 4.5.

The dollar cost averager has achieved a terrific 951 percent total real return on his $100,000 investment, seeing it grow to $1,051,008. The Market Timer has attained a 1,235 percent total return. Although he only invested $84,000 to begin with,

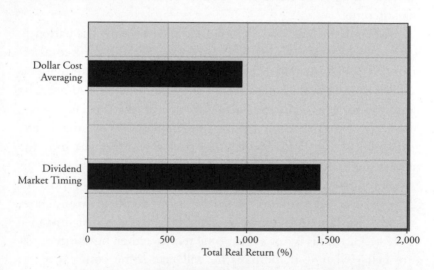

**Figure 4.5   Dollar Cost Averaging versus Dividend
Market Timing, 1902–2001**

his account swelled to $1,121,786—a 30 percent better return than his friend. This gives him a nice cushion for social security. Plus, he still has money sitting at interest in the bank, awaiting the next investment opportunity.

1977–2001

It's déjà vu all over again when we examine the dividend story over the past 25 years. The dollar cost averager slogs $100 a month into the market at the end of every month. The Market Timer invests $200, but only when the dividend yield on the S&P 500 is above its 15-year moving average, as shown in Figure 4.6.

The familiar pattern reasserts itself. Using dividends as his guide, the Market Timer buys stocks through the mid-1980s, and

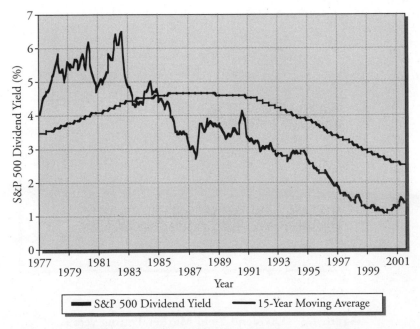

Figure 4.6   S&P Dividend Yield, 1977–2001

then holds his hand thereafter. Figure 4.7 shows how their investments performed over the quarter-century.

The dollar cost averager spent $30,000 over this period for a take of $75,059: a total return of 150 percent. Using the dividend yardstick as his guide, the Market Timer has grown $17,600 into $68,123, for a total real return of 285 percent. Since he was putting his cash into riskless T-bills when he wasn't investing it, the Market Timer also has an additional $14,651 (principal + inflation-adjusted interest) awaiting his next investment opportunity. He has more money overall: $82,774.

The dividend yield is another useful tool Market Timers with no special training can use to gauge the value of the stock market as a whole. When dividends are generous, the market is priced low. You can look up the current dividend yield of the S&P 500 in *Barron's* "Market Laboratory" every week. As a rough guide, you might want to compare it with its average over the past 25 years, which is 3.4 percent.

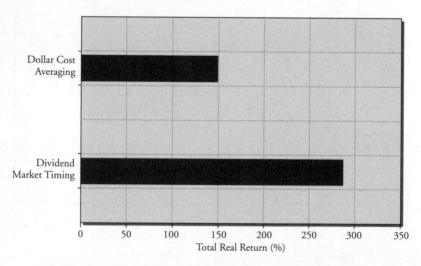

Figure 4.7   Dividend Yield Market Timing versus Dollar Cost Averaging, 1977–2001

But, you may ask, "Aren't dividends passé?"

During the high-growth era of the 1990s, it was almost bad taste to speak of dividends. These were for stodgy old bricks-and-mortar establishments that had not shifted their operations to the Web yet. Hip CEOs would not think of parting with so much as a nickel of their companies' earnings. They even disdained to speak of earnings, period. It was all about gaining market share. Now that these stocks have blown up in people's faces like exploding cigars, the mood is shifting to one of nostalgia for old-fashioned *money*. People are beginning to yearn for the security, the final reality, of a dividend payment, and desperate CEOs may be forced to issue dividends once again to lure investors back into the market. This, by the way, would exert a salutary discipline on corporate officers and directors. If they have to come up with actual cash to pay their stockholders, they will have to avoid game playing and moving around imaginary stacks of cash to show an illusory success. The repeal of double-taxation of dividends by the government would go a long way toward simplifying things for everyone.

Chapter Five

Fundamental Value

The approaches we have taken to time the market so far have all been based on some external characteristic of the stock market: its price, earnings, or dividend yield. What if we take a different tack? We could send in a fleet of accountants to determine the total value of the companies that make up the S&P 500, and then compare this number to the price for which they are selling on Wall Street. This would give us a direct measure of whether the market was over- or underpriced.

There are two ways to do this. One would be to figure out what it would cost to replace each company if it were gone. Professor James Tobin, Nobel Prize winning economist at Yale University, espoused this approach. He divided a company's replacement cost (i.e., the cost of its physical assets, licenses, copyrights, patents) into the total market price of all its stock, and this ratio became known as Tobin's Q. It is a direct measure of value and can be calculated for the stock market as a whole as well as for the individual companies that comprise it. A high ratio indicates that the market is pricing companies above their replacement cost and indicates that the stock market is expensive. A low Tobin's Q says that the stock market is priced conservatively.

A different path to determining fundamental value is to look at a company's balance sheet and subtract all of its liabilities from all of its assets. This is also a measure of what a company is worth: its *book value*. This supposedly tells us its "real" as opposed to its stock market value. When we divide this number into the aggregate value of all its outstanding stock, we obtain its price-to-book ratio. The price-to-book ratio can be computed for a single company or for a group of companies, such as the S&P 500 Index. A high price-to-book ratio suggests the market is expensive, while a low price-to-book ratio indicates that valuations are attractive. This is a second direct measure of whether the stock market is high or low.

Both approaches have their detractors. Some critics claim that Tobin's Q focuses on tangible assets like land and machinery, but underestimates the value of intellectual property and brand names. For example, the name Coca Cola or Walt Disney is worth something in the global market, even if all the bottling plants and theme parks disappeared tomorrow.

On the other hand, depending on how it is calculated, the price-to-book ratio can be susceptible to accounting vagaries. Because of tax depreciation schedules, Ford might carry a factory on the books at zero dollars, yet the land and plant could be worth millions of dollars on the open market. Sprint may show assets of fiber optic cables and computers and switches that cost hundreds of millions of dollars as assets on the books, yet have difficulty getting more then a few pennies on the dollar for them at a fire sale tomorrow. In fact, this has happened to the telecom industry in recent years.

The fact that neither system is perfect should not blind us to the truth that, in most situations most of the time, Tobin's Q and price-to-book give us a pretty good estimate of value, especially when we focus on the stock market as a whole rather than on one or another idiosyncratic company within it. This conviction is reinforced by the fact that the correlation between these two measures is extremely high: +.99 since 1977. When Tobin's Q is high, the price-to-book ratio is high, and when Tobin's Q is low, the price-to-book ratio is low.

The reason Tobin's Q and price-to-book fell out of favor as measures of stock market valuation is that, during the Internet boom, both metrics said stocks were too expensive. Thus, stockbrokers could not use them as stock-selling tools. Since stocks kept going up, the valuation measures appeared to be wrong—quaint holdovers from the old bricks-and-mortar economy. Then stocks stopped going up, in fact, they went down severely, and people began to rediscover the neglected wisdom of considering fundamental valuation measures such as Tobin's Q and price-to-book in weighing stock purchases.

Benjamin Graham put fundamental value at the top of his stock-selection list, recommending that investors purchase a stock when it was priced at no more than 65 percent of the company's underlying net asset value. Professor Henry Oppenheimer reported on the results of Graham's method in the *Financial Analysts Journal* in 1986:

- For each of 13 years from 1970 to 1983, Oppenheimer looked at the behavior of the U.S. stocks that met Graham's 65 percent criterion, holding each cohort of these low price-to-value stocks for one year, and then selling them to buy next year's group of low price-to-value stocks. He found these stocks returned an annual mean of 29 percent during this period versus 12 percent for the stocks from the New York and American Stock Exchanges overall.
- In a study running from 1967 to 1984, Roger Ibbotson divided the stocks on the New York Stock Exchange into equally weighted deciles according to their price-to-book value. He found that the mean annual return of the most expensive price-to-book decile averaged 6 percent in the year that followed, while those stocks with the lowest price-to-book value garnered a 14 percent annual return.
- DeBondt and Thaler sorted the stocks of the New York and American Stock Exchanges by their price-to-book ratio into quintiles during the 1960s and 1970s and then went back to see how these groups performed over the subsequent four years. The quintile with the lowest price-to-book ratio had appreciated 41 percent more than the stock market as a whole over this period, while the quintile with the highest price-to-book ratio returned 1 percent below the market over the following four years.
- Another research team, Lakonishok, Vishny, and Shleifer, arranged the stocks of the New York and American Exchanges into deciles according to their price-to-book ratios from 1968 to 1990. Five years later, they found the

highest price-to-book ratio stocks returned 9 percent annually on average, while the low price-to-book decile stocks returned 20 percent annually.

- The investment firm of Morgan Stanley found the same pattern held true in their database of international stocks. Outsized returns went to those stocks that were priced cheaply relative to their net asset values when compared to their higher priced brethren in developed markets around the world.

Could we use these measures of fundamental value, not to assist with individual security selection, but to help us time the market as a whole?

Figure 5.1 highlights the correspondence between Tobin's Q and the stock market over the past century.

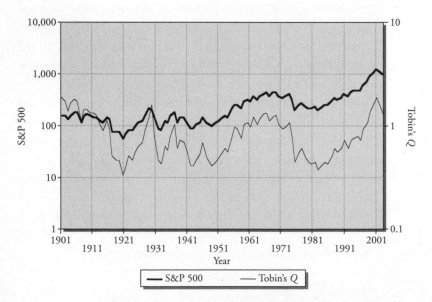

Figure 5.1   S&P 500 and Tobin's Q

To transform Tobin's *Q* into a market timing predictor, we compare its current value with its long-term (15-year) trend line, as shown in Figure 5.2. Our plan is to buy the stock market whenever Tobin's *Q*—the fundamental value of all its companies divided into their current price—is below its long-term moving average.

Our methodology here is the same as before:

1. Sort the years of the century according to whether Tobin's *Q* is above or below its 15-year moving average.
2. For all the years when Tobin's *Q* is above the trend line (and therefore the market is expensive), assume we bought the S&P 500 at the end of each of these years.
3. Track how the S&P 500 did in the following 5, 10, 15, and 20 years, calculating the total real returns for each period.

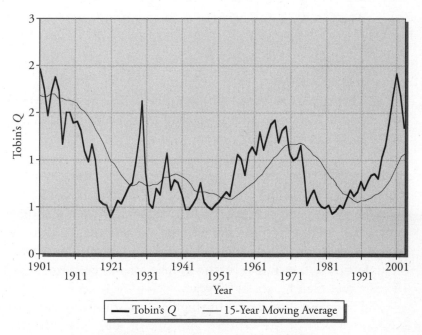

Figure 5.2   Tobin's *Q*, 1902–2001

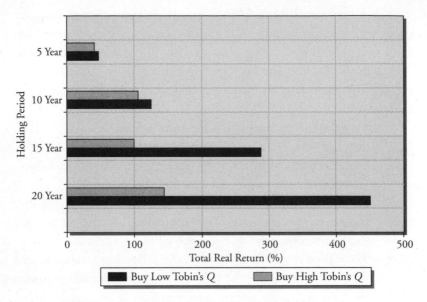

Figure 5.3   Tobin's Q Market Timing, 1902–2001

4. Average the returns for each holding period: 5, 10, 15, and 20 years.
5. Then repeat steps (2) through (4) for all the years when Tobin's Q is below its 15-year moving average and stocks appear to be cheaply priced.

Figure 5.3 plots the average outcomes from having bought the market when Tobin's Q was high or low relative to its 15-year trend line across the century. Buying Tobin's Q when it is low does better over every time period, and the advantages become progressively greater the further out we go. By contrast, note how the unfortunate Buy-High-Tobin's-Q investor was even worse off 15 years later than he was at 10 years.

Did it make a difference how high or low Tobin's Q was? We sorted each year of the century into one of four quartiles, according to where Tobin's Q stood relative to its long-term average. As before:

1. The quartile with the highest 25 percent of scores we labeled "High," the next 25 percent of scores was labeled "Above Average," the first 25 percent of scores below the long-term mean were called "Below Average," and the quartile containing the years with the lowest 25 percent of Tobin's Q ratios was labeled "Low."
2. We checked how the years in each quartile performed as times to invest. We assumed that an investor bought the S&P 500 Index at the end of each of the years in each quartile, held the Index for 20 years, and then sold it, calculating the total real returns generated.
3. We averaged all the 20-year investment returns obtained for each quartile.

Figure 5.4 reveals the outcomes. Not only does it matter *whether* Tobin's Q is above or below its long-term moving average, it matters a great deal *to what degree* it is above or below this line.

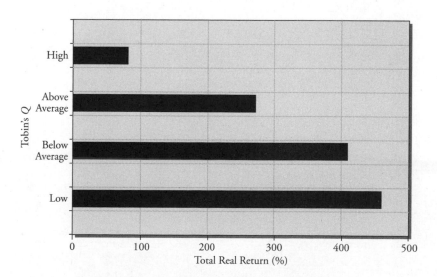

Figure 5.4   Twenty-Year Total Real Return by Tobin's Q Quartile When Purchased

**Table 5.1   Total Real Returns Based on Tobin's Q
When Purchased**

Year	Tobin's Q	+5 Years (%)	+10 Years (%)	+15 Years (%)	+20 Years (%)
1902	Above Average	−11	45	0	43
1903	Low	51	51	22	69
1904	Above Average	32	11	−2	64
1905	High	4	27	−33	75
1906	Above Average	5	20	−16	97
1907	Low	64	12	61	305
1908	Low	0	−19	12	310
1909	Low	−16	−26	24	229
1910	Low	22	−36	68	186
1911	Low	14	−21	87	72
1912	Low	−31	−2	148	67
1913	Low	−19	12	311	186
1914	Low	−12	48	291	189
1915	Low	−47	38	135	209
1916	Low	−30	64	51	318
1917	Low	43	261	143	315
1918	Low	38	409	254	439
1919	Low	67	342	227	409
1920	Low	163	346	488	472
1921	Low	135	116	498	257
1922	Low	152	69	189	204
1923	Low	268	156	290	269
1924	Below Average	165	96	205	242
1925	Below Average	70	124	118	266
1926	Above Average	−8	154	52	147
1927	High	−33	15	21	72
1928	High	−30	6	0	19
1929	High	−26	15	29	58
1930	Above Average	32	28	115	143
1931	Below Average	177	65	168	355
1932	Low	71	80	155	426
1933	Below Average	52	44	71	240
1934	Below Average	56	75	114	443

Table 5.1 *(Continued)*

Year	Tobin's Q	+5 Years (%)	+10 Years (%)	+15 Years (%)	+20 Years (%)
1935	Above Average	−3	64	84	399
1936	High	−40	−3	65	297
1937	Below Average	5	49	208	450
1938	Below Average	−5	12	124	473
1939	Below Average	12	37	248	540
1940	Low	68	89	413	613
1941	Low	63	176	565	1,022
1942	Low	42	193	422	812
1943	Low	19	136	505	804
1944	Below Average	22	210	470	793
1945	Above Average	13	205	324	639
1946	Below Average	70	309	590	729
1947	Low	107	268	544	933
1948	Low	99	410	662	974
1949	Low	154	367	630	670
1950	Below Average	171	277	556	518
1951	Above Average	141	306	388	485
1952	Above Average	78	212	400	473
1953	Above Average	156	283	440	358
1954	High	84	188	204	96
1955	High	39	142	128	91
1956	High	69	103	143	118
1957	High	75	180	221	118
1958	High	49	111	79	51
1959	High	57	65	6	44
1960	High	74	64	38	71
1961	High	20	44	29	18
1962	High	61	84	25	54
1963	High	41	20	1	50
1964	High	5	−32	−8	33
1965	High	−6	−21	−2	53
1966	Above Average	20	7	−2	107
1967	High	15	−22	−4	73

(continued)

Table 5.1   *(Continued)*

Year	Tobin's Q	+5 Years (%)	+10 Years (%)	+15 Years (%)	+20 Years (%)
1968	High	−15	−28	7	83
1969	Below Average	−36	−13	26	167
1970	Low	−16	4	63	147
1971	Low	−10	−18	73	183
1972	Below Average	−32	−17	51	157
1973	Low	−16	26	115	251
1974	Low	35	96	314	429
1975	Low	24	94	195	453
1976	Low	−8	93	215	457
1977	Low	23	123	279	739
1978	Low	49	155	316	987
1979	Low	45	206	292	1,123
1980	Low	57	138	346	813
1981	Low	111	245	508	805
1982	Low	81	208	582	?
1983	Low	71	179	630	?
1984	Low	111	170	742	?
1985	Below Average	52	185	483	?
1986	Above Average	64	189	330	?
1987	Above Average	70	276	?	?
1988	High	63	326	?	?
1989	High	28	299	?	?
1990	High	88	284	?	?
1991	High	77	163	?	?
1992	High	121	?	?	?
1993	High	161	?	?	?
1994	High	212	?	?	?
1995	High	105	?	?	?
1996	High	49	?	?	?
1997	High	?	?	?	?
1998	High	?	?	?	?
1999	High	?	?	?	?
2000	High	?	?	?	?
2001	Above Average	?	?	?	?

The investor who bought the market when its stocks were selling at a significant premium to their replacement costs was cruelly punished for his mistake.

Table 5.1 on pages 78 to 80 shows how investing during each year of the century profited according to the Tobin's *Q* level at the time. As above, each year falls into one of four quartiles according to how much Tobin's *Q* was above or below its 15-year moving average at year's end. Then we measured the total real returns that resulted from buying stocks at the end of each year.

LUMP SUM INVESTING USING FUNDAMENTAL VALUE

An investor who suddenly comes into a pot of money has two choices regarding the stock market. He can follow the "Stocks-for-the-Long-Run" approach and throw his money at the market immediately, on the theory that in the long run the stock market will more than make up for any initial bumps. Alternatively, he can keep his powder dry until he finds the stock market to be at a price of his liking.

Imagine that two investors each have a lump sum of $50,000 to deploy into the stock market during the twentieth century. One uses Tobin's *Q* to time his purchase, while the other buys at the end of any year when he feels like it. As before, we calculated all possible 20-year returns over the century to see how these two investors fare on average. In the case of the "any-time" investor, his returns are the average that would have been obtained across all rolling 20-year periods. For the Market Timer, we take those returns only from years when Tobin's *Q* is below its 15-year moving average, that is, when stocks appear to be cheap.

Twenty years later, the Market Timer has seen his fortune grow 450 percent, to $275,000, some 34 percent better than his colleague who failed to take the *Q*-tip. His $50,000, by contrast, has only grown to $218,500, an average total real return of 337 percent.

DOLLAR COST AVERAGING USING FUNDAMENTAL VALUE

The investor who dollar cost averaged $1,000 into the stock market at the end of each year of the century would have discovered his $100,000 initial investment (in year 2001 dollars) blossoming to $1,051,008 by the end of 2001, a total real return of 951 percent. The Market Timer, who assumed he would be investing only about half the time, doubles his bets, putting his money on the table when Tobin's Q is below its long-term average. This happy fellow would have invested $108,000 and seen his brokerage statements fatten to $1,569,933 for a total real return of 1,354 percent, some 42 percent better than his cohort. Their relative returns are shown in Figure 5.5.

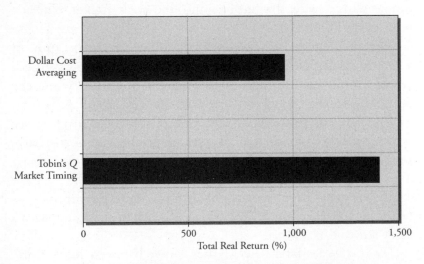

Figure 5.5 Dollar Cost Averaging versus Tobin's Q Market Timing, 1902–2001

1977–2001

Turning to the past 25 years, we are going to pull a switch. For the century as a whole, we looked at the annual Tobin's Q ratio (market value/replacement cost) as our guide. One reason for doing this was that the data exist, thanks to the diligence of Professor Stephen Wright and Andrew Smithers, whose book on Tobin's Q *Valuing Wall Street* we highly recommend. Unfortunately, we do not have monthly data for Tobin's Q for the past 25 years, and as far as we have found, no one else does, either. So, for the more recent period, we will turn to the other direct measure of fundamental value, the price-to-book ratio (market value divided by [assets minus liabilities]), with which Tobin's Q is closely correlated.

One more confession: Other researchers may fare better, but the price-to-book data we found were only available going as far back as 1977. As with our other metrics, we wanted to begin in 1977 and compare its status with its historical moving average. But that meant we really needed the data going back to 1962. How did we fill in the blanks? We used a statistical technique known as *regression analysis* to reconstruct estimates prior to 1977, basing them on Tobin's Q for the period 1962–1976. Fortunately, the extremely high correlation between the Tobin's Q ratio and the price-to-book ratio (statistically, 98 percent of the variability of one is accounted for by the other) suggests that we can be confident in these estimates.

The price-to-book ratio is available monthly, even weekly. Its widespread availability gives the price-to-book ratio an advantage over Tobin's Q going forward.

Figure 5.6 shows the price-to-book ratio of the S&P 500 from 1977 to 2001 alongside its (partially reconstructed) 15-year moving average. Our strategy is to buy the stock market when its companies are being valued cheaply, when the price-to-book line is below its own 15-year moving average.

Our two investors will once again partake of the market differently. Starting in 1977, the dollar cost averager spends $100 on

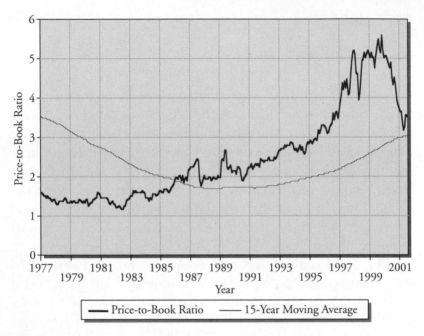

Figure 5.6   S&P 500 Price-to-Book Ratio, 1977–2001

stocks at the end of each month. The Market Timer buys $200 worth of the S&P 500 Index only at the end of any month when the market is cheap according to its price-to-book ratio.

Three hundred months later, here is the scorecard: The dollar cost averager has sunk $30,000 (year 2001 dollars) into the market and seen his portfolio grow to $75,059 by the end of 2001, for a total return of 150 percent. The Market Timer invested only $22,000 over this interval, but this has now grown to $83,435, for a total real return of 279 percent—some 86 percent better. Their returns are shown in Figure 5.7. These do not even include the $9,453 the Market Timer currently has lounging in T-bills.

Clearly, fundamental measures of equity value have a great deal to say about the future. Comparing the price of the S&P 500 Index with either the book value of the underlying assets or their replacement costs proves to have considerable predictive utility.

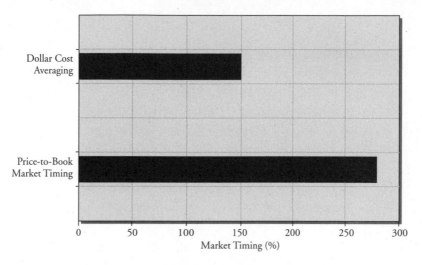

**Figure 5.7   Dollar Cost Averaging versus
Price-to-Book Market Timing**

Although the price-to-book ratio is published weekly in *Barron's,*
we have used a data series from Standard & Poor's that uses a
slightly different method to make the calculations. You can find
this at www.barra.com/research/fundamentals.asp. As a rough
guide, the mean price-to-book ratio for the S&P 500 for the past
25 years has been 2.3.

We now turn to three more factors to consider when pricing
the market: price-to-sales, price-to-cash flow, and the yield
from the bond market.

Chapter Six

Bonds, Price-to-Cash Flow, Price-to-Sales

From a stockbroker's point of view, there is only one invest- ment in the world, and that is stock. Stocks are beautiful, and people should buy stocks at all times.

Investors, however, have a choice as to how to deploy their capital, including whether to deploy it in the stock market at all. You can watch CNBC all day long and scarcely be aware that there are other entire classes of investment-grade instruments. One asset class that competes side by side with stocks for our dol- lar is *bonds*.

A bond is an IOU issued to raise capital. Corporations sell bonds when they think they can use the capital to earn more money than it will cost them to service the debt. Remember that when people trade stocks, no money goes back to the company after the initial public offering. The only sources of new rev- enues are from earnings, from the sale of more stock (which di- lutes the value of the stock outstanding), or borrowing money via a bond issue.

The conventional wisdom is that people buy stocks for growth and buy bonds to add ballast and dampen out the volatile ups and downs of the stock market. While this shaves the total re- turn, it offers a smoother ride.

There are about 27 different kinds of bonds, but they all come down to lending money in the expectation that it will be re- turned with interest. In that respect, they may be compared with stocks, which also take our money today and let us participate in an earnings stream going forward. With a share of stock, we are a part owner of a company, while with a corporate bond, we lend the company money, typically at a fixed rate of interest. Each in- vestment has distinct features. Stocks hold out the prospect of growth (although the price of bonds may also increase, if interest rates fall and render the bond's income stream more valuable, or if the issuer's ability to pay off the bond becomes more secure). By the same token, bonds generally fall in value if interest rates rise. Bondholders also will be in line ahead of stock owners should the company fail and its remaining assets be distributed.

A bond usually has a set coupon that translates into a current yield, while a share of stock has an earnings yield (standing the price/earnings ratio on its head gives us the earnings/price ratio). By examining the yields on the stock market to those available in the bond market, we can compare them head-to-head. The other factors we have discussed so far (price, earnings, dividends, fundamental value) are internal to the stock market. The bond/stock earnings comparison theoretically allows us to hold up the bond market as an external yardstick for judging the value of the stock market.

Some observers have tried to promote the relationship between stocks and bonds to a precise mathematical formula that would calculate when stocks are fairly valued. This is the so-called *Fed Model,* and it is "so-called" because no one has ever proved that the Federal Reserve Board is guided by it. One version of the Fed Model posits that the stock market is correctly priced when its forward-looking earnings yield is equal to the interest rate on the long-term government bond. Accordingly, if stock earnings yields are higher than this, it is time to buy stocks. If the government bond yield is higher, we should buy bonds, since stocks are overpriced and headed for a fall.

Put this way, the Fed Model is silly. No one knows what future earnings will be. Just because someone is willing to make up a number when asked does not mean it will come true. It is difficult enough trying to get a company's board of directors to tell us what last year's earnings were with any reliability. The indeterminacy of future earnings makes the Fed Model a flaccid yardstick at best. To guess the future in this way is a study in frustration.

A second difficulty with the Fed Model is more subtle. Why should the yield on stocks be compared to *government* bonds? Government bonds are considered to be virtually risk-free, because they are backed by the full faith and credit of the United States. Since the Department of the Treasury owns and runs the printing presses and the IRS, there is an excellent chance that you will get your money back, at least at its nominal value.

Since the Fed Model compares an investment that is riskless with one that has substantial risk and has to pay a substantial premium to offset that risk, it should come as no shock that stocks come out looking like terrific buys most of the time. The reason why this model refuses to die is that it is basically a sales tool for stockbrokers.

One of your humble authors studied economics at Yale under the tutelage of Professor Henry Wallich, the man credited with inventing said Fed Model. The cunning difference, however, is that Professor Wallich's version used trailing instead of future earnings, and compared them with the yield on long-term corporate bonds instead of risk-free Treasury bonds. Put in its original way, the model makes much more sense. Now we are comparing the earnings yield on stocks with the coupon rate these same companies pay on their bonds. Both have risks, as both are subject to cycles and market forces. This comparison sharpens the focus considerably. It is like saying a stock can be viewed as a bond with its earnings yield as the coupon rate. If the stock's yield is too low compared with yields available elsewhere (i.e., the bond market), people will stop buying stocks and their price will fall, until they become competitively priced once more. If the stock market's earnings yield is overly generous compared with other available yields, people will snap up equities, bidding up the price in the process, until the stock's earnings yield once more moves into equilibrium with the yield available on bonds with similar risk characteristics.

One of Benjamin Graham's stock screening rules was to select stocks whose earnings yields were twice the coupon rates of their bonds. This is excellent advice. Unfortunately, the last time this was true of the stock market as a whole was 1957.

Figure 6.1 charts how the earnings yield from the S&P 500 has stood against the coupon rate from Moody's top-rated AAA 10-year corporate bonds over the past century.

For roughly the first two-thirds of the century, there seems to be no relationship between stock earnings yields and corporate bond coupon rates, although stock yields were very high compared with recent years. Then, in the last third of the century, they started moving in sync.

What happened? Was the premium for the extra risk of holding stocks simply too high earlier? Did the fact that the U.S. government artificially pegged treasury yields low from 1941 to 1951 distort the credit markets? Did the scourge of inflation in the 1960s and 1970s, as well as the government's attempt to combat it by using interest rates, cause people to price stocks and

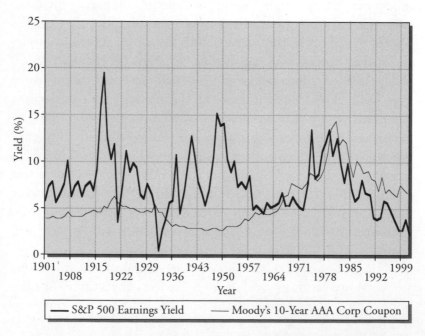

Figure 6.1   Stock Earnings versus Bond Yields, 1901–2001

bonds differently? We don't know, but the effects of inflation on all interest-bearing instruments were dramatic.

Since it was almost always a good time to buy stocks by this model before 1966 (except for 1932, when the price/earnings ratio went askew), these earlier years are useless as indicators. We know that many of them in fact were terrible years to buy stocks. This means we will have to focus on more recent history to determine whether the relative yields from stocks and bonds can be used to time the stock market.

1977–2001

Figure 6.2 holds a magnifying glass up to the earnings yields from S&P stocks and the dividend yield from Moody's AAA-rated 10-year corporate bonds over the past 25 years.

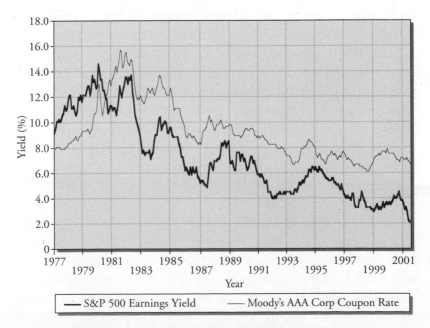

Figure 6.2 Stock and Bond Yields, 1977–2001

Our strategy will be to buy stocks when they are attractively priced compared to bonds, that is, when the earnings yield on stocks is higher than the coupon yield available from highly rated 10-year corporate bonds.

The price-sensitive Market Timer dollar cost averages $200 a month into the S&P 500 Index on every such occasion. The dollar cost averager puts $100 into the market every month come what may. Twenty-five years later, what do we find?

The dollar cost averager has put in $30,000 and now has a portfolio worth $75,059—a total real return of 150 percent. The bond Market Timer only found a few occasions in which to invest, watching his $8,800 turn into $30,681—although for a far better total real return of 249 percent. In accordance with a stock versus bond timing model, his remaining money waiting in corporate bonds would now be worth an inflation-adjusted $49,900, for a total edge of $5,522.

However, because the bond timing method only put him in the market 15 percent of the time over these years, he missed a number of good investment opportunities. Taken by itself, this version of the Fed Model can be a problematic way to buy stocks because of the scarcity of buying occasions it presents. For your own research, the earnings yield of the S&P 500 is published every week in *Barron's*. You can look up the current yield available from Moody's AAA 10-year bonds on the Internet at www.economy .com (and elsewhere), or, if you prefer, use the yield on the *Barron's Best Grade Corporate Bond Index Yield* as a convenient proxy.

PRICE-TO-CASH FLOW RATIO

Now that investors have come to distrust management's earnings statements, some have turned to a different method to judge the value of a stock. A corporate income statement starts with total revenues or sales and then deducts various expenses to arrive at net earnings. These expenses might be anything: rent, wages, taxes, amortized depreciation of equipment, costs associated with financing debt, the cost of the company's art collection, loans to the CEO for a Telluride chalet, and so on.

The farther down the list you go, the more chances there are for the numbers to be suspect. On the other hand, *cash flow* purports to be what is left over from the company's sales when you subtract only the actual cost of generating those sales in the first place. Cash flow is sometimes defined as earnings before interest, taxes, depreciation, and amortization (the notorious EBITDA, also known as Earnings-Before-Bad-Stuff). This gives us considerable pause, because in the real world, bad stuff happens. In fact, this ratio favors stocks that have plenty of bad stuff, like telecom companies with huge depreciations that are overhung with debt.

Still, cash flow is what pays for everything else. While we would never use cash flow to recommend an individual stock, we grudgingly acknowledge that it may be useful as a thermometer for the stock market as a whole, where the idiosyncrasies of many different companies are washed out. If creative accountants and chief financial officers distort a stock's earnings, at least the cash flow might give us a more revealing picture about what kind of revenues are flowing from core business operations.

We get the *price-to-cash flow ratio* by dividing the total cash flow of the S&P 500 Index into its total market capitalization. When the ratio is low, it suggests that we are getting a lot of cash flow for our dollar of stock; when it is high, it suggests that we are only getting a trickle and therefore stocks are expensive. There is even some research to back this up:

- Writing in the *Journal of Portfolio Management,* Michael Keppler looked at the price-to-cash flow ratio for 17 countries over almost 20 years. Four times a year, he sorted the countries into quartiles based on their price-to-cash flow and measured how these countries' markets performed in the three months following. His finding: The countries with the lowest price-to-cash flow ratio outperformed the others.

- Professors Lakonishok, Vishny, and Shleifer ranked all the companies in the New York and American Stock Exchanges into deciles based on their price-to-cash flow ratios on an annual basis from 1968 to 1990. They studied how these various portfolios performed five years later. Once again, the decile with the highest price-to-cash flow ratio had the lowest average annual return five years later (9 percent), while the decile with the lowest price-to-cash flow ratio had the best average annual return (20 percent).

- James O'Shaughnessy examined a group of large stocks similar to the S&P 500. He selected the 50 stocks with the lowest price-to-cash flow ratios in 1951 and rebalanced his holdings annually. By 1994, they had achieved an annual compound return of 16.5 percent, compared to 12.6 percent for stocks in general.

Instead of using the price-to-cash flow ratio to select individual stocks, we wanted to see whether this ratio could successfully time the purchase of the market as a whole. Our strategy would be to compare the current price-to-cash flow ratio with its 15-year moving average to judge whether stocks appear cheap or fully valued.

As with the price-to-book ratio, we only had monthly statistics going back to 1977. This meant we had to reconstruct the missing data from 1962 to 1977 to get our 15-year moving average started. We used a regression analysis to derive the probable price-to-cash flow from the earnings yields during this earlier period.

Figure 6.3 shows the price-to-cash flow ratio from 1977 to 2001 alongside its 15-year moving average.

Once again, two individuals invest in the stock market over 25 years. One, a dollar cost averager, buys $100 worth of the S&P 500 Index every month, come what may. The other, a Market Timer, puts $200 a month into the market, but only at the end of those months when the price-to-cash flow ratio is below its long-term trend line. How do their investments perform?

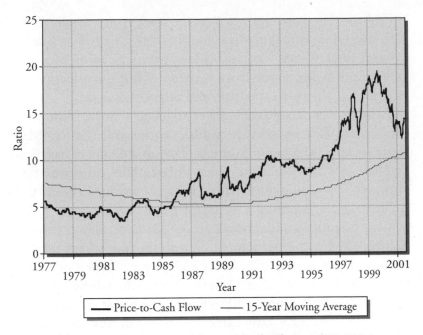

Figure 6.3   S&P 500 Price-to-Cash Flow, 1977–2001

As of the end of 2001, the pure dollar cost averager has spent $30,000 (year 2001 dollars) over the years, and now has, as usual, $75,059 to show for it: a total real return of 150 percent. The Market Timer has spent $21,400 over the same length of time, and it has now grown to $81,544: a total real return of 281 percent. In addition, he is sitting on a pile of cash worth $10,134 for investing on a rainy day. Price-to-cash flow is worth watching.

PRICE-TO-SALES

Why go even halfway down the income statement? Why not just take the top line, the company's total sales over the past four quarters? If a company has sales, at least you know money is coming in the door. Divide total sales into the total market capitalization of the stock (or divide the price of a share of stock by the annual sales per share) and we have the stock's price-to-sales ratio. This tells us how much revenue the company brings in per dollar of stock price. When the ratio is low, we are gleaning plenty of sales for our dollar, so the stock is cheap. When the price-to-sales ratio is high, sales are expensive, and the stock is dear.

This is a perfectly terrible way to value a stock. Who cares about sales? What matters are *profits*. A nationwide chain of bagel stores recently went out of business. They sold plenty of bagels, so that was not the problem. Their price-to-sales ratio was fine. However, it was estimated that each bagel cost them several dollars to make. This proved a recipe for going broke.

The point is: A dollar of sales is not the same all over town. A farmer selling soybeans, competing with the lowest cost producers on the planet, might be lucky to squeeze a penny or two of profit out of a dollar's sales. A biotech company with a sexy new designer drug might profit 30 cents out of a dollar in sales.

The price-to-sales ratio came into vogue during the Internet era. Because the dot-coms had no earnings, and in fact were black holes into which money was being poured, the price/earnings ratios were untenable. Even the price-to-cash flow metric was difficult to sell, because core operations were burning through far more cash than they generated. In this desperate environment, price-to-sales ratios at least showed there *were* sales. The ratio came to stand as a back-of-the-envelope proxy for market share. The theory went that these companies would grow market share first, at astonishing rates, and eventually profits would catch up. Having a huge amount of debt served to leverage the price-to-sales ratio even more, alchemically transmuting a liability into an asset. It was a great party while it lasted.

The price-to-sales ratio becomes more meaningful when applied to a basket of stocks like the S&P 500 Index, many of whose stocks have at least some solidity and history:

- In their excellent publication titled *What Has Worked in Investing?* the value-oriented investment firm of Tweedy,

Brown & Company notes that a low price-to-sales ratio is often correlated with other valuation measures, such as a low price/earnings ratios and a low price to net asset value.
- O'Shaughnessy looked at a large stock index similar to the S&P 500 and found that picking the lowest price-to-sales ratio stocks in 1952 and rebalancing them every year through 1994 trounced the overall index, 18.9 percent to 14.6 percent. Price-to-sales performed better than any other valuation measure he studied.

As with price-to-cash flow and price-to-book, we only have monthly data on price-to-sales going back to 1977, so we reconstructed our moving average data for the beginning years of our data series using a regression analysis similar to the one we employed for the price-to-cash flow ratio. The results are shown in Figure 6.4.

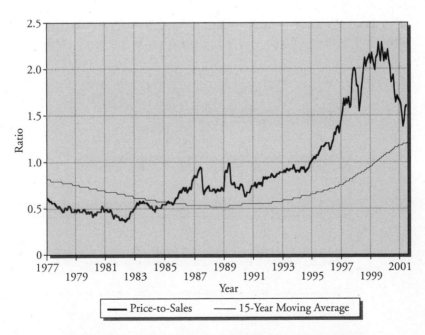

Figure 6.4   S&P 500 Price-to-Sales, 1977–2001

As before, we consider the stock market to be desirably valued when the price-to-sales ratio of the S&P 500 Index is below its 15-year trend line, and the market to be overvalued when it is above this moving average.

Proceeding on this assumption, a Market Timer puts $200 into the S&P composite index every month during the past 25 years when the market meets this valuation criterion. His non-Market Timing dollar cost averaging friend puts $100 into the market every month. How do their final portfolios compare?

The dollar cost averager has put $30,000 into the market over this period, and his brokerage statement shows a bottom line of $75,059—as always, a total real return of 150 percent. The price-to-sales timer has results nearly identical to those of the price-to-cash flow timer: having spent $21,400, and now he has an account worth $81,591, for a total real return of 289 percent (plus $10,134 of cash left over in T-bills or $13,285 if he put his cash into government bonds).

Figure 6.5 shows the comparative returns of our three newest Market Timing signals over the past quarter century compared

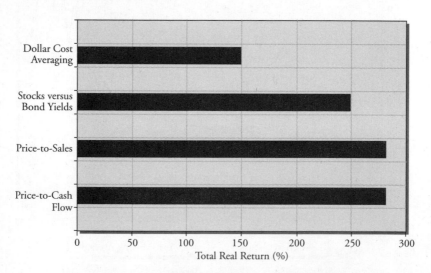

Figure 6.5   Market Timing, 1977–2001

with those of the dollar cost averager. With the caveats noted, these factors would seem a desirable addition to our Market Timing arsenal.

The price-to-sales ratio and the price-to-cash flow ratio can be looked up every month online at www.barra.com/research/fundamentals.asp. For the past 15 years, the price-to-sales has averaged 1.2 and the price-to-cash flow has averaged 10.4.

Now we will see how all these factors we have studied work in combination.

Chapter Seven

Combining Factors for
Superior Returns

We have marched through a century of data with four factors to predict long-term investment performance. Let us see how they stack up against each other, and how they work in combination.

We began by considering the case of investors who each had money to dollar cost average into the S&P 500 Index at the end of every year throughout the century:

1. The first invested at the end of every year.
2. The second invested only in those years when none of our timing signals was indicating a buying opportunity.
3. The third invested according to price (at the end of those years when the current inflation-adjusted price of the S&P 500 fell below its 15-year moving average).
4. The fourth invested guided by the price/earnings ratio (buying when the price/earnings of the Index fell below its 15-year moving average).
5. The fifth invested according to the market's dividend yield (buying when dividends were above their 15-year moving average).
6. The sixth invested according to fundamental value (buying when the ratio of price to replacement cost was below its 15-year average).

Their returns are shown in Figure 7.1.

The investor who used any of these four Market Timing signals to time his purchases over the course of the entire century did at least 39 percent better than the individual who simply sunk his money into the S&P 500 Index every year, and 445 percent better than the hapless mis-Timer who happened to plunk down his money only during the years when none of our buy signals were flashing. The superior performance of price,

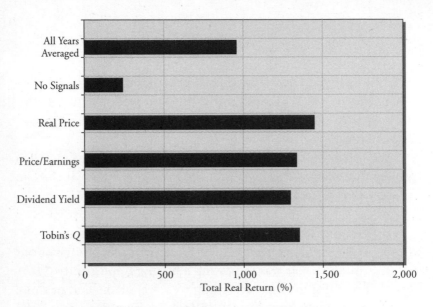

Figure 7.1   Market Timing, 1902–2001

the simplest metric of all, is attributable to the fact that it is a
key ingredient in the other three measures. This is fully compat-
ible with the efficient marketer's contention that price contains
all available information about the status of securities at any
given time.

Figure 7.2 reflects the hypothetical results of dollar cost averaging $1,000 a year (2001 dollars) into the S&P 500 Index over
the century according to *how many* timing signals were flashing at
the end of each year:

- "All Years" means the investor bought the index every year
  no matter what the market timing signals said.
- "No Signals" refers to those 36 years when no signal was
  indicating a buy.
- The remaining bars on the graph show the results of dollar
  cost averaging in those years when one or more, two or

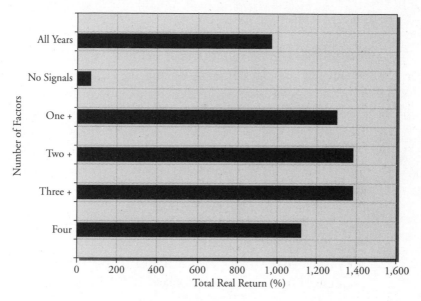

Figure 7.2   Dollar Cost Averaging versus Market Timing, 1902–2001

more, three or more, or all four signals were showing stocks to be attractively valued.

    Buying when the market was reasonably priced by any of these four indicators gave you at minimum a 39 percent better total real return on your investment than buying every year.

    Note the falloff that occurs when investing in years when all four criteria tell us that valuation levels are attractive. Is this an anomaly? No. There were only 27 such years in the century, and 12 of them clustered near the end of the period we were measuring. They simply have not had enough time to rise as high as those years earlier in the century when all four signals were flashing, thus bringing down the average. Given sufficient time, we predict that this "All Four" indicator's returns will rise to match or even exceed the others.

LUMP SUM INVESTING

We examined how a lump sum investor might have fared had he put $50,000 into the stock market during the past century, depending on whether or not he timed the market according to one of the templates. To summarize our methodology:

1. We sorted the century according to which years each factor we looked at was signaling a buy (by virtue of being above or below its 15-year moving average).
2. For the years when the market was cheap by each of these valuation measures, we bought the S&P 500 at the end of these years.
3. We calculated the total real return for the S&P 500 over the subsequent 5, 10, 15, and 20 years. If 1902 was a buy, we

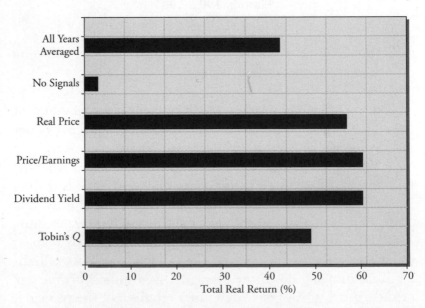

Figure 7.3 Five-Year Total Returns

measured how stocks bought then would have performed had they been sold in 1907, 1912, 1917, and 1922. For 1903, we sold in 1908, 1913, 1918, and 1923, and so on.

4. We averaged the returns for each factor for each holding period: 5, 10, 15, and 20 years.

5. Finally, we did the same thing for two points of comparison: the total real returns over every 5, 10, 15, and 20 year period we could measure (All Years Averaged), and once more for those specific years when none of our market timing signals indicated a buy (No Signals).

The results are presented in Figures 7.3 through 7.6.

Benjamin Graham said that in the short run, the market is a voting machine, but in the long run, it is a weighing machine.

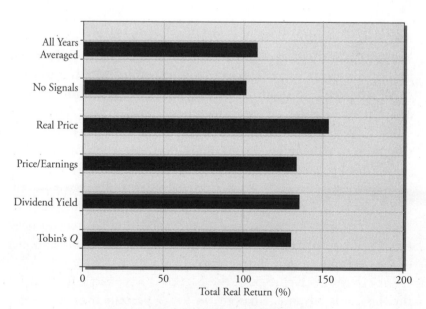

Figure 7.4   Ten-Year Total Returns

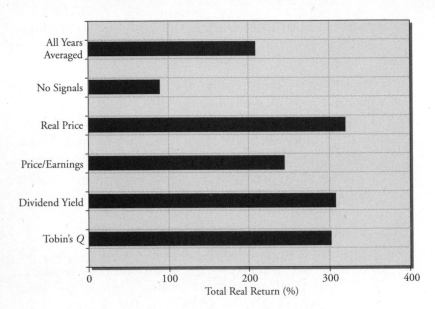

Figure 7.5   Fifteen-Year Total Returns

We now can quantify Graham's observation. Figure 7.3 shows that at five years out the market timing wizardry only makes a small difference. It is only 11 percent ahead of the random model and 5 percent ahead of the years where none of the factors was salient. This helps explains why most of the research on market timing is so dismaying: In the short run, the stock market is a high school popularity contest where true value is overlooked.

However, as Figure 7.4 shows, by 10 years, things have started to turn around. The lump sum Market Timer is now doing 16 percent better than his devil-may-care colleague, and 31 percent better than the accidental market mis-Timer who invested when none of the criteria were signaling a buy.

At 15 years (Figure 7.5), the Market Timer has left them in the dust. His advantage has grown to 39 percent over the every year investor and 319 percent better than the investor who jumps in during one of the bad years by our criteria.

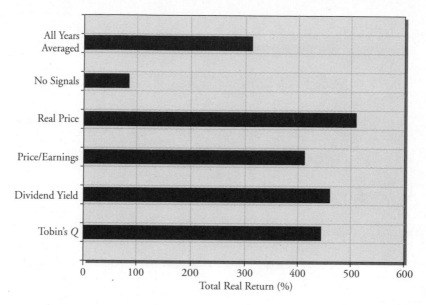

Figure 7.6 Twenty-Year Total Returns

At 20 years (Figure 7.6), the Market Timer's pace continues. His returns are 39 percent better than the random investor and a whopping 577 percent better than the mis-Timer.

COMBINED FACTORS

We counted how many of our Market Timing factors (price, price/earnings ratio, dividend yield, Tobin's Q) were signaling a buy each year. In some years, there were no signals flashing. In other years, there might be two, three, or even all four. We sorted the years according to how many buy signals were green: zero, one, or more; two or more; three or more; and four. Then we looked at how investing in each of these conditions performed 5, 10, 15, and 20 years later, averaging these results for each group. For comparison, we also plotted how the stock market performed

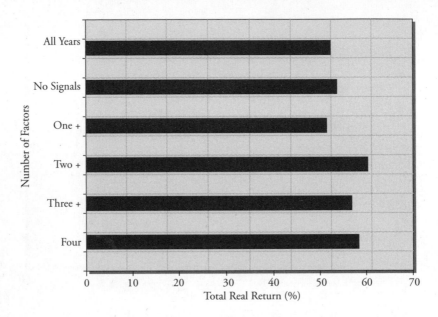

Figure 7.7   Combined Factors at 5 Years

on average over all these time periods. The results are shown in Figures 7.7 through 7.10.

On average, five years out from the point of initial investment, there is little benefit to market timing. If two or more signals were hit during the year you made your initial investment, though, you do about 11 percent better than without this benefit. However, noise in the data overwhelms the signals.

In Figure 7.8, at 10 years past the point of initial investment, you are 32 percent better off having followed two timing signals, on average, than none at all, and 17 percent better than the average of all years.

In Figure 7.9, 15 years past the point of initial investment, the years when there was at least one market timing signal present are doing fully 19 percent better than purchasing the market at random and 258 percent better than buying a year when none of the signals was giving a green light.

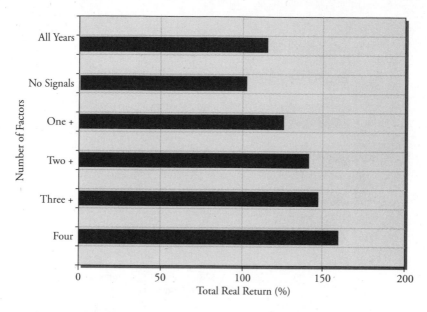

Figure 7.8   Combined Factors at 10 Years

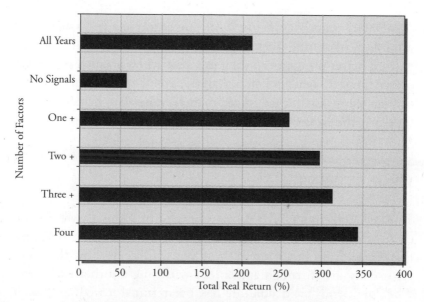

Figure 7.9   Combined Factors at 15 Years

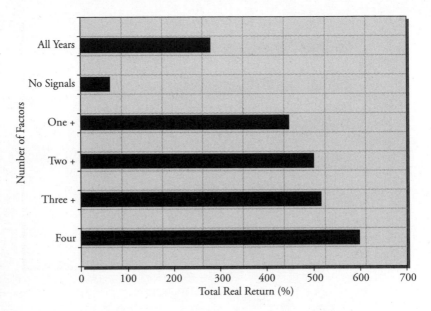

Figure 7.10   Combined Factors at 20 Years

Twenty years later (Figure 7.10), investing in a year when there was one market timing signal giving you a green light puts you 501 percent better off than investing in a year when no such signal was present, and 23 percent better than the average of all years. Market timing using established stock market valuation benchmarks is suddenly the conservative, long-term investor's best friend.

YEAR BY YEAR

Tables 7.1 through 7.10 show what the buy signals were from each of our market timing strategies from 1902 to 2001, and the results from investing in these years. Observe how the criteria usually are in rough agreement with one another each year. The Dividend Yield column has been transformed so that it matches the others (a high dividend yield corresponds to a low market valuation and a low dividend yield points to a high market value).

1902–1913

The century began with a wave of prosperity under President McKinley and the conservatives in control of the government. Note how these good times were not particularly good times to invest in the stock market (except during the recession of 1903), in terms of the long-term real return on investment. Then, in 1907, there was a severe banking panic. Large trust companies were lending money in competition with commercial banks, but without the banks' reserve requirements. Several of them went bankrupt that summer, taking down some stock brokerages with them. A run on the banks began, and a nationwide recession loomed. In short, it was a great time to buy stocks. That is what J.P. Morgan did, even as he was leading the nation out of the crisis.

Table 7.1   Market Valuations, 1902–1913

Year	Price	P/E	Dividends	Tobin's Q	20 Years Later (%)
1902	High	Low	Above Average	Above Average	43
1903	Above Average	Low	Low	Low	69
1904	High	Below Average	High	Above Average	64
1905	High	Low	High	High	75
1906	High	Low	Above Average	Above Average	97
1907	Below Average	Low	Low	Low	305
1908	High	Below Average	Below Average	Low	310
1909	High	Low	Below Average	Low	229
1910	Above Average	Low	Low	Low	186
1911	Above Average	Above Average	Low	Low	72
1912	Below Average	Below Average	Low	Low	67
1913	Low	Low	Low	Low	186

1914–1922

The world is at war. The Communist Revolution in Russia. Postwar inflation. Then, in 1920-1922, a Depression caused by severely mistaken and restrictive monetary policy. Great buying opportunities, all.

Table 7.2 Market Valuations, 1914–1922

Year	Price	P/E	Dividends	Tobin's Q	20 Years Later (%)
1914	Low	Above Average	Low	Low	189
1915	Below Average	Low	Above Average	Low	209
1916	Low	Low	Low	Low	318
1917	Low	Low	Low	Low	315
1918	Low	Low	Low	Low	439
1919	Low	Low	Above Average	Low	409
1920	Low	Low	Low	Low	472
1921	Low	High	Below Average	Low	257
1922	Low	Above Average	Above Average	Low	204

1923—1929

A new era of never-ending prosperity begins under President Coolidge. This time it is different: The business cycle has been defeated. Cars, household appliances, and a housing boom. The growth of advertising and installment buying. Stocks are on everyone's lips, and margin requirements are minimal. Virtually any stock purchase now results in an overnight profit. In spite of appearances, 1927 and onward turn out to be a terrible time to buy. In 1929, the market collapses.

Table 7.3   Market Valuations, 1923–1929

Year	Price	P/E	Dividends	Tobin's Q	20 Years Later (%)
1923	Low	Below Average	Below Average	Low	269
1924	Below Average	Below Average	High	Below Average	242
1925	Above Average	Below Average	High	Below Average	266
1926	Above Average	Below Average	High	Above Average	147
1927	High	High	High	High	72
1928	High	High	High	High	19
1929	High	Above Average	High	High	58

1930–1939

The Federal Reserve fails to supply desperately needed credit, tightens money, the Smoot-Hawley Tariff is enacted effectively extinguishing foreign trade, and the nation sinks into a depression. (See *Ferris Bueller's Day Off* for a further discussion by one of your authors.) By 1932, the market has lost at least five-sixths of its value. Congress responds by . . . raising taxes. Roosevelt takes over, but despite innumerable new government programs and acts and agencies, the New Deal is unable to do anything about the Depression, and makes matters worse. Doom and gloom. Capping it off,

Table 7.4   Market Valuations, 1930–1939

Year	Price	P/E	Dividends	Tobin's Q	20 Years Later (%)
1930	High	High	Above Average	Above Average	143
1931	Below Average	High	Low	Below Average	355
1932	Below Average	High	Below Average	Low	426
1933	Above Average	Above Average	High	Below Average	240
1934	Below Average	Above Average	High	Below Average	443
1935	Above Average	Below Average	High	Above Average	399
1936	High	Below Average	High	High	297
1937	Below Average	Low	Low	Below Average	450
1938	Above Average	Below Average	Above Average	Below Average	473
1939	Below Average	Low	Below Average	Below Average	540

there is a sharp recession within the Depression in 1937–1938. By 1939, the total output of the U.S. economy is less than it was in 1929. In sum: a sensational time to buy stocks.

1940–1945

World War II. Pearl Harbor. German Submarines in New York harbor. With the lend-lease program, we begin sending goods to the Allies. Deficit spending and mobilization for the war effort finally pulls us out of the Great Depression. The atom bomb. More great buying opportunities.

Table 7.5   Market Valuations, 1940–1945

Year	Price	P/E	Dividends	Tobin's Q	20 Years Later (%)
1940	Below Average	Low	Low	Low	613
1941	Low	Low	Low	Low	1,022
1942	Low	Low	Below Average	Low	812
1943	Below Average	Low	Above Average	Low	804
1944	Below Average	Low	Above Average	Below Average	793
1945	High	Low	High	Above Average	639

1946–1953

Military spending continues in peacetime as the Cold War begins. The Korean War. Time to buy.

Table 7.6   Market Valuations, 1946–1953

Year	Price	P/E	Dividends	Tobin's Q	20 Years Later (%)
1946	Below Average	Low	Above Average	Below Average	729
1947	Low	Low	Below Average	Low	933
1948	Low	Low	Low	Low	974
1949	Below Average	Low	Low	Low	670
1950	Above Average	Low	Low	Below Average	518
1951	High	Below Average	Below Average	Above Average	485
1952	High	Below Average	Above Average	Above Average	473
1953	High	Below Average	Below Average	Above Average	358

1954–1972

The postwar economic expansion and prosperity under Eisenhower and Kennedy. The Great Depression is now a distant memory, and people step into the market once more. Even those recessions that do occur are remarkably mild. The stock market copes well with the inflation caused by the Vietnam War. As with previous periods of prosperity, short-term returns are good, but long-term returns are not.

Table 7.7   Market Valuations, 1954–1972

Year	Price	P/E	Dividends	Tobin's Q	20 Years Later (%)
1954	High	Above Average	High	High	96
1955	High	Above Average	High	High	91
1956	High	Above Average	High	High	118
1957	High	Above Average	Above Average	High	118
1958	High	High	High	High	51
1959	High	High	High	High	44
1960	High	High	High	High	71
1961	High	High	High	High	18
1962	High	High	High	High	54
1963	High	High	High	High	50
1964	High	High	High	High	33
1965	High	Above Average	High	High	53
1966	High	Below Average	Above Average	Above Average	107
1967	High	Above Average	High	High	73
1968	High	Above Average	Above Average	High	83
1969	Above Average	Below Average	Below Average	Below Average	167
1970	Above Average	Above Average	Below Average	Low	147
1971	Above Average	Above Average	Above Average	Low	183
1972	High	Above Average	Above Average	Below Average	157

1973–1985

The OPEC oil embargo, compounded by wildly expansionist monetary policy, leads to rampant inflation, and paper assets of all kinds (except cash) are killed. The stock market loses half its value. For the price-sensitive investor: another buying opportunity.

Table 7.8   Market Valuations, 1973–1985

Year	Price	P/E	Dividends	Tobin's Q	20 Years Later (%)
1973	Low	Low	Below Average	Low	251
1974	Low	Low	Low	Low	429
1975	Low	Low	Low	Low	453
1976	Low	Low	Below Average	Low	457
1977	Low	Low	Low	Low	739
1978	Low	Low	Low	Low	987
1979	Low	Low	Low	Low	1,123
1980	Low	Low	Low	Low	813
1981	Low	Low	Low	Low	805
1982	Low	Low	Low	Low	?
1983	Below Average	Above Average	Below Average	Low	?
1984	Below Average	Low	Below Average	Low	?
1985	Above Average	High	High	Below Average	?

1986–1995

The long boom. Apart from a recession in 1991, an unprecedented stretch of economic good times for America begins. Immediate investment results are excellent; long-term results: unknown.

Table 7.9   Market Valuations, 1986–1995

Year	Price	P/E	Dividends	Tobin's Q	20 Years Later (%)
1986	High	High	High	Above Average	?
1987	High	High	High	Above Average	?
1988	High	Above Average	High	High	?

Table 7.9   *(Continued)*

Year	Price	P/E	Dividends	Tobin's Q	20 Years Later (%)
1989	High	High	High	High	?
1990	High	High	High	High	?
1991	High	High	High	High	?
1992	High	High	High	High	?
1993	High	High	High	High	?
1994	High	Above Average	High	High	?
1995	High	Above Average	High	High	?

1996–2001

The Federal Reserve, believing that the Internet and Telecom revolutions have permanently raised productivity, pumps liquidity into the system while everyone cheers. The money goes directly into the stock market, creating a bubble, which bursts in 2000 and is still being worked off as of late 2002, with the S&P 500 down over 40 percent and counting. Long-term results are unknown, but the outlook for equities going forward is not sanguine.

Table 7.10   Market Valuations, 1996–2001

Year	Price	P/E	Dividends	Tobin's Q	20 Years Later (%)
1996	High	High	High	High	?
1997	High	High	High	High	?
1998	High	High	High	High	?
1999	High	High	High	High	?
2000	High	High	High	High	?
2001	High	High	High	Above Average	?

Investors are commonly assured that, with a long-term time horizon, stocks are the safest place to be. However, over a 10- or 15-year period, you can lose money in stocks. Even after 20 years, with all dividends reinvested and accounting for inflation, it is possible to still be sitting behind the starting line.

The total return we receive from stocks is not just a function of the numerator: the money we get when we sell. Equally vital is the denominator: the price we paid, our cost basis. Buy into the frenzy of a market peak, when stocks are sizzling, and your money can cool its heels for the next two decades or even longer.

HOW HIGH? HOW LOW?

We took each year of the past one hundred and gave it a score ranging from 0 to 12 according to how expensive the market looked at the time by our valuation measures. If the stock market appeared to be valued cheaply by all four criteria, the year rated a zero (0 + 0 + 0 + 0 = 0). If the stock market looked like

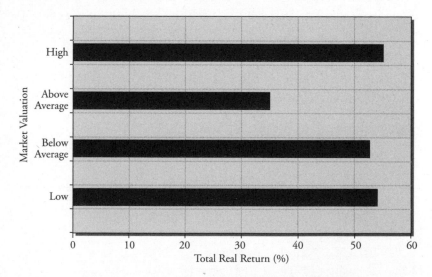

Figure 7.11   Market Valuations 5 Years Later

it was priced low on three of the four criteria, but was merely Below Average on the fourth, it rated a one $(0 + 0 + 0 + 1 = 1)$. If the year were Below Average on two of the criteria while Low on the other two, it rated a two $(0 + 0 + 1 + 1 = 2)$—as it did if it were Low on three of the criteria but Above Average on the fourth $(0 + 0 + 0 + 2 = 2)$. And so on, for all of the years. If the stock market seemed expensive by all four criteria, the year got a 12 $(3 + 3 + 3 + 3 = 12)$.

With each year graded, we separated them into quartiles according to how high or low their grades were. We called the 25 percent of the years that looked the cheapest Low, the next 25 percent Below Average, the next 25 percent Above Average, and finally the 25 percent that appeared to be most expensive by our measures, High.

We went back through the century and looked at how all of the years in each quartile performed over the subsequent 5, 10, 15, and 20 years. Then we averaged the total real returns obtained by each group. The results are presented in Figures 7.11 through 7.14.

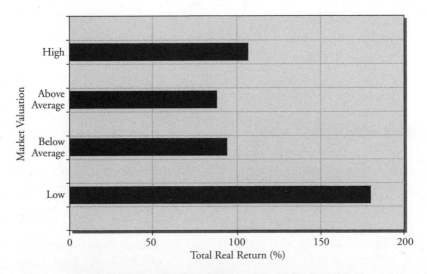

Figure 7.12   Market Valuations 10 Years Later

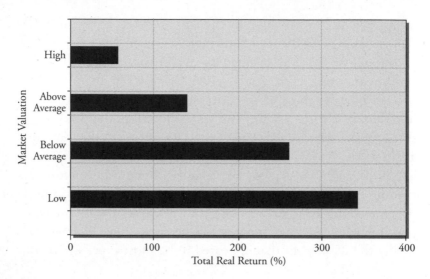

Figure 7.13   Market Valuations 15 Years Later

If you see a meaningful pattern in Figure 7.11 (page 122), you have better glasses than we do. Five years out, it does not seem to matter how high or low our timing signals judge the market to be. Short-term market "noise" drowns out everything else.

Even at 10 years (Figure 7.12), there is not much structure to the data. However, the quartile where the stock market valuation appeared the lowest at the time of investment now dramatically outperforms the others.

Suddenly, at 15 years (Figure 7.13), the scales fall from our eyes. The same quartiles of years that gave such confusing, mixed signals five years later suddenly sort themselves out. The more expensive the market appeared to be at the time when we bought, the worse our returns. The cheaper it looked, the better our returns are today.

Twenty years later (Figure 7.14), we have the same story, only more so. It is as if a magician appeared and lifted his cape from the stock market. We cannot tell you if the market is going to be

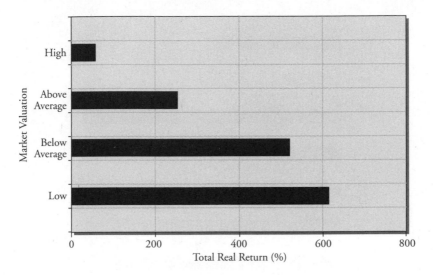

Figure 7.14   Market Valuations 20 Years Later

up or down in five years, and cannot even tell you that much about 10 years out, but now it suddenly appears to be possible to look squarely at the stock market today and come up with a pretty good guess of whether it is a good time to buy looking out 15 or 20 years.

It is not Prometheus, it is not Tiresias, it is not Superman's X-ray vision, but this may be about as close as we are going to get where the stock market is concerned.

1977–2001

For the recent past, we added the three new factors (stock yields versus bond yields, price-to-sales, and price-to-cash flow) to the ones we had running throughout the century, while substituting the price-to-book ratio for the Tobin's Q ratio used earlier.

Figure 7.15 shows how these factors fared when timing monthly stock purchases over the past 25 years, both compared to

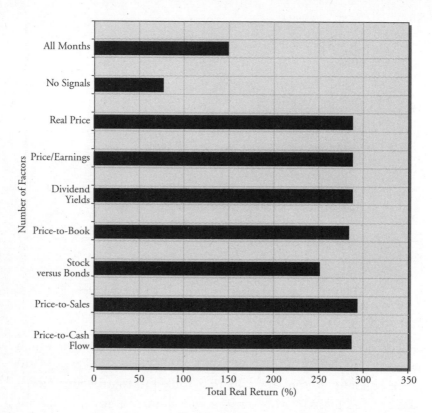

Figure 7.15 Market Timing, 1977–2001

the Non-Market Timer who bought every month no matter what (All Years) and the Mis-Timer who bought only in the months when no timing signals were present. Notice how the Market Timer using any of our seven factors secures an 87 percent improvement on average over the widely touted dollar cost averaging method.

When we combine the factors, and use a signal on any one of them to select months to buy stocks, the results are similar (Figure 7.16). The more timing signals are popping their corks, the merrier the results. *Exception:* Waiting for all seven criteria to agree before buying actually caused a perceptible falloff in total

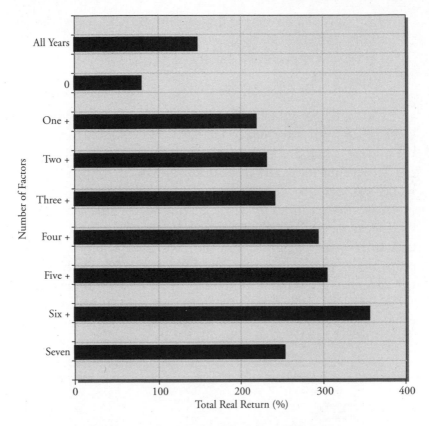

Figure 7.16   Market Timing, 1977–2001

performance. This is not a mystery. It is attributable entirely to what might be termed the opportunity costs of the infrequent bond market signal. Given the rarity of this signal, you might choose to disregard it altogether.

Next, we sorted each of the months into one of four quartiles according to how high or low it ranked according to all of the timing signals:

- We gave each month a grade using the same 0–3 scale we previously employed for rating the years.

• We dollar cost averaged into the market and sorted the results according to whether the timing signals suggested the
market was priced High, Above Average, Below Average,
or Low.

Once again, the total returns from dollar cost averaging over
the past 25 years have neatly arranged themselves according to
the evident valuations at the time of purchase (Figure 7.17).

These data make the mechanism by which Market Timing
works transparently clear. Market Timing does not allow us to
jump on a spaceship to the stars. First, it boosts our total returns
by helping us sidestep those years when stocks are most overvalued. In 36 years out of the last 100, stocks were fully valued by
every one of the four criteria. The Market Timer owes his superior investing performance to taking a pass on investing at these
occasions, despite the prevalent Wall Street fever to get in the action. Successful investing is not about picking the hottest stocks
or mutual funds, the savviest broker or the portfolio manager on

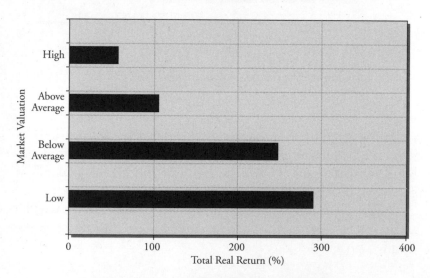

**Figure 7.17   Market Timing and Dollar
Cost Averaging, 1977–2001**

the cover of *Money* magazine, who are stone cold a few months later in any event. It is not about some cunning "black box" space-age simulation of the laws of physics to achieve unheard of, brilliant results. *It is about avoiding crushing mistakes.* Market Timing helps us avoid the dumb years to invest, so that we do not overpay for stocks in the first place. Second, it calls our attention to stock market opportunities during periods when everyone is running from stocks like the sky is falling, and so helps us buy low. It is that straightforward.

In fact, it works so well that the Non-Market Timer's returns are governed by exactly the same mechanism: He does well if by lucky fate his purchases are concentrated when the market cheap, and poorly if he buys when it is expensive. While the dollar cost averager at least gets the benefit of the good years to leaven the bad, the lump sum investor does not. For these individuals, investing in a bad year when the market is priced high can be costly indeed.

A SLIGHTLY TECHNICAL FOOTNOTE ON MARKET TIMING AND RISK

Stock market risk is commonly equated with something called *standard deviation,* a statistical measure of variability from the mean. Standard deviation is simple to measure, making it easy for graduate students to grind out papers on the topic. Investors, though, are more concerned about the prospect of losing money.

Beta is a measure of risk pegged to the standard deviation of the S&P 500 Index as a whole, which is defined as having a benchmark beta of one. One of the beauties of comparing investments in the S&P 500 with each other as we have done is that both should have the same beta.

Do they have the same risk? Not necessarily. Because we are measuring different time periods (e.g., all of the rolling 10-year periods from 1902 to 2001 versus a specific subset of these), their standard deviations (their "risks," if you will) can differ.

Figure 7.18 is a different kind of graph than we have shown previously. On the left axis, it plots total return. The higher you go, the better the investment has performed. The axis along the bottom plots the level of risk (standard deviation). The farther to the right you go, the riskier the investment was, or, more precisely, the more it fluctuated in the course of securing the returns it achieved. This type of chart allows us to see the trade-offs between risk and reward for a given investment. The ideal investment would be very high on the Total Return axis and all the way to the left on the Risk axis. Unfortunately, since investors are being paid precisely to take risk, this ideal investment does not exist. What we can do, however, is compare the relative risk/reward trade-offs of real-world investments.

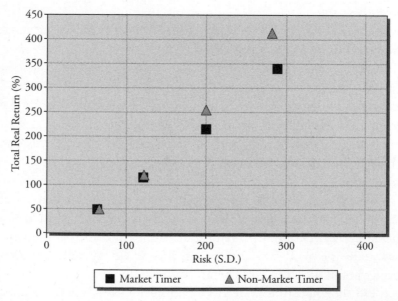

Figure 7.18   Risk versus Return 5, 10, 15, and 20 Years Later

On this grid we have placed the 5-, 10-, 15-, and 20-year outcomes for the Market Timer (the triangle) and the Non-Market Timer (the square). The 5-year outcomes for both are nearly on top of each other in the lower left-hand corner. The next group up the diagonal is the 10-year outcomes, still on top of each other. By 15 years, they have separated: the Market Timer has significantly higher returns with very slightly more risk. At 20 years (the upper right triangle and square), the Market Timer gets to have his cake and eat it, too: he has far superior returns, with less risk than the Non-Market Timer.

Another measure of risk is called the *Sharpe ratio,* after its creator, Nobel economist William Sharpe. The Sharpe ratio subtracts the risk-free return obtainable over the period (90-day T-bills) from the actual returns an investment obtains, and then divides the difference by the standard deviation. The larger the Sharpe ratio, the better, since this means that you are getting a higher risk-adjusted return for your money. T-bills have a Sharpe ratio of zero. There is no point putting your dollars at risk unless you can secure a greater risk-adjusted return than this.

The Sharpe ratios for the 5-, 10-, 15-, and 20-year groups when at least one factor signaled a buy are shown in Figure 7.19. These are compared with all possible 5-, 10-, 15-, and 20-year Sharpe ratios over the same period, such as might have been obtained by the Non-Market Timer. According to the Sharpe ratio, there is no risk-adjusted advantage for the 5-year investor, but as time goes on, the Market Timer does better not only absolutely, but on a risk-adjusted basis.

Remember that standard deviation is a neutral measure of how much these returns varied from the mean, and not necessarily the same thing as risk. Not all deviations are created equal. If you get outsized returns on the upside one year, this is wonderful news, not bad. Only the deviation down (and the prospect of losing money that it portends) keeps investors tossing and turning at night. The standard deviations of the Market Timer and the Non-Market Timer are not symmetrical. The returns from the

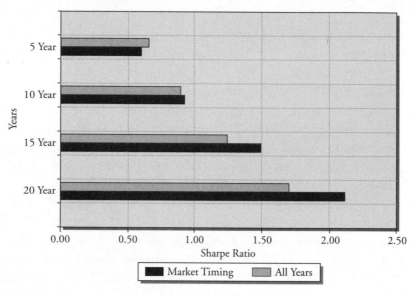

Figure 7.19   Sharpe Ratios

long-term Market Timer have a standard deviation that represents more deviation going up, while the Non-Market Timer has more deviation going down.

The case of the dollar cost averagers is more complex. Again, both the Market Timer and the Non-Market Timer are only investing their stock portfolios in the S&P 500, and so these both by definition might have a beta of one. But since the Market Timer is doubling his bets on occasion, there are times when he may have more money in the stock market than the Non-Market Timer, and hence has more to lose or gain. At other times, the Market Timer may hold treasury bills (which by definition have a beta of zero), either exclusively or in combination with holding stocks. This lowers the risk of his portfolio compared to that of the all-stock-holding dollar cost averager. Over a long time, the Market Timer's risk should be lower, if the past century is any guide. This is because dollar cost averaging can ultimately be broken down into a series of discrete lump sum investments (whether annual or monthly), and so should have similar risk/return profiles to the lump sum investments graphed earlier.

Statistics aside, the real reason valuation-based stock market timing lowers risk is because it lowers your cost basis, which means you have less chance of losing real money. There is less to fear from falling stocks if you bought them when they were inexpensive. The risk of stocks is that you may drastically overpay and end up under water for a decade or two. Also, the Market Timer often has some money in risk-free cash, which lowers his downward risk profile. Market Timing is the difference between pricing stocks and throwing darts.

Now we will look at how to put this theory into practice, turning our information into ammunition.

Chapter Eight

Using Market Timing

Wall Street's know-nothingism is disingenuous. Do not ignore price when you buy stocks.

The securities business wants to flatter you into thinking that you are a long-term investor, even if you only started investing this morning. If they can convince you that you are a long-term investor, price will not matter, since, as every schoolchild "knows," stocks always go up in the long run. That way, they can sell you stocks today. It is a sales tactic.

Long-term investor is not an appellation to be tossed around lightly. It means you have stayed the course through 20 or 30 years of the worst kind of crises, personal, political, and economic. You lost half your money and went home to have dinner with the wife and kids, still holding your stocks. Or, the stock market was going up 5 percent a day, and all the while you held onto your bond position. If you are a long-term investor, which is to say, someone who has actually held stocks for a long time— you look like Arnold Schwarzenegger toward the end of one of his action movies: beat up, bloodied, covered with mud, clothing torn, with a look of grim determination on your face. While we hope to have shown a certain limitation to the blind buy-and-hold strategy, let us be clear. If you have been in the stock market for 20 or 30 years, you have courage.

Warren Buffett is a long-term investor. Yet nobody watches a nickel more closely than he does. Being a long-term investor is not a license to buy assets at whatever price is being asked. If you overpay to begin with, Mr. Market is going to teach you a lesson. You are going to feel like a chump and be tempted to bail at the first sign of turbulence. Most of the so-called "long-term investors" the financial services industry caters to are out of the market within two or three years.

Although "Stocks for the Long Run" is by no means incompatible with value-based market timing, it is usually mistranslated as "Ignore the Price Tag" by the financial securities industry. The salesman's ABC is "Always Be Closing," and "Stocks for the Long Run" becomes a slogan to sell you stocks right now, not on some tomorrow that may never come.

Often, we are only too happy to be told to ignore price, because we have no idea how to value stocks. This is a paradox of our investment age: We are admonished to be in stocks at all times, but at the same time we have no idea what they are really worth. We know the price of every stock but the value of none.

In an era when the dominant intellectual mini-movement has been deconstructionism, perhaps it is unsurprising that people came to view the passing parade of numbers on the stock ticker as merely another self-referential text, unconnected to anything outside itself. Wall Street has harvested a generation of nominalists who think stocks are worth what the quotron says, rather than realists who look for their underlying value.

Nietzsche called himself the philosopher with a tuning fork because he tested every proposition to make sure it rang true. We need to be investors with tuning forks, testing each transaction to make sure it rings true as well. Our tuning forks are the basic valuation measures we have described.

Market Timing should be used within the context of a conservative investment program. This means, first of all, that it should fit into your overall plans and goals, taking into account your total assets and liabilities, your age, your responsibilities and obligations, your cash flow, and other factors unique to your life. It is shortsighted to worry about market timing if you do not have health insurance or if you are carrying a $20,000 Visa card balance on an income of $500 per week.

We recommend the following principles to guide your investment decisions going forward.

1. BUY LOW

The time to buy stocks is when at least one of the signals shows that they are relatively cheap. It is even better if more than one signal is flashing. But historically, even just one green light is dramatically better than none. Had you consulted our Market Timing signals before buying, you would have bought into every one of the top 15 years for subsequent 20-year stock performance since 1926, and completely sidestepped the 15 worst years. These measures are for real.

2. SELL HIGH

The century began with the S&P at 7, and ended at 1148, close to its all-time high. From that perspective, any intervening sale might be considered a mistake, in the sense that if one had waited longer, the S&P 500 might have been higher still.

While Wall Street believes that stock ownership is a valuable end in itself, most people have some use in mind for the money they have temporarily entrusted to securities. If we must sell our stocks, it is undoubtedly better to do so when they are fully priced by these measures. Thumb through the tables in this book again, but this time imagine that you are selling High rather than buying Low. You will see how much better you typically will have done from the standpoint of 10 or 20 years in the future.

3. DIVERSIFY, DIVERSIFY, DIVERSIFY

Did we say diversify? While the financial press endlessly trumpets stocks and the latest hot mutual funds, *the conservative investor should always remain highly diversified—both among and within asset classes.* This means owning cash, bonds, real estate, and stocks.

Cash

By cash, we mean ready money available in your checking or savings account, short-term certificates of deposit, T-bills, or money market accounts. Some people despise cash since it usually pays a low rate of interest—barely keeping pace with inflation. However, we feel that cash is a beautiful thing. When the stock market goes down 20 percent, 30 percent, 40 percent, cash just keeps looking better and better. Its value is that it stays the same, even when other assets are tanking. This is itself a huge saving. Stock millionaires can be wiped out in days. Do not become one of these guys. Cash: It's a good thing.

A word of warning: It is a common, if unfortunate, practice for brokerage firms to mistreat their customers by paying almost no interest on money market accounts. Get the highest after-tax interest you can. Every week, *Barron's* and the *Wall Street Journal* publish lists of the highest yielding money market accounts, or you can find them online at www.ibcdata.com and elsewhere. Find a money market fund that pays high interest without the gimmick of a special promotional rate.

At all times, we think you should hold plenty of cash to cover current expenses and a six-month cushion for emergencies in an account where you can get your hands on it. There may well be times when you want to hold more cash than this, even considerably more. There is nothing wrong with keeping 10 percent of your assets in cash. No one from *Investor's Business Daily* will come to arrest you.

Real Estate

For most Americans, their house is their most significant asset. Some financial advisors recommend ignoring your personal residence. This is a mistake. We live in California. Many of the rich people we knew in the 1990s who owned big stock portfolios are not so rich anymore. It seems like the people we know who are rich today are the ones who own their houses. By next year, this may change, but for now, they are sitting pretty.

There are some bad things about houses, so let's get them out of the way right now: They are a relatively illiquid, nondiversified asset. They have high transaction costs to buy and sell. They are expensive to maintain. Their value can go down, and fast. That said, there are many wonderful things about houses, and we must sing their praises. Houses provide a tremendous sense of psychological peace and shelter. They shield us from the elements and from the harshness of the world outside. They hold their value beautifully over long periods of time and keep up with inflation.

If all this were not enough, the government believes that you ought to own one, and is willing to cut you a significant tax break if you take the plunge. Your mortgage interest will in all likelihood be completely tax deductible, meaning that you can borrow money cheaply to buy your house over time. When you sell your house, you will not have to pay any capital gains taxes on the first million dollars of profit if it is your primary residence and you have lived there two years. If all this were not enough, you also get the imputed rental value of your house tax-free. The $25,000 or $250,000 it would cost to rent a house like yours every year is money that you get to pocket instead, untaxed. For all these reasons, we love our homes.

You should own your personal residence. We also like Real Estate Investment Trusts (REITs), which invest in baskets of income properties, and diversify a portfolio while providing a stream of income. Preferably, these are housed in tax-sheltered accounts.

Houses have a price/earnings ratio, just as stocks do. The earnings here are the house's rental value (after maintenance). If your house is worth $240,000, and renting it out would clear $1,000 a month after expenses, it has a price/earnings ratio of 20 ($240,000 / $12,000). You can use this price/earnings ratio as a barometer to judge how expensive neighborhoods are, both in relation to each other as well as to themselves, historically. As with stocks, we do not recommend that you buy your house in the cloud cuckoo land of a real estate market bubble.

The price of your house will fluctuate. But you will not have cheating CEOs running your house and defrauding you, nor will you find your house to be worthless paper. You can always live in it. That is saying a lot.

Bonds

There are many different types of fixed-income investments. Bonds vary according to their time horizon and their overall credit quality. Long-term bonds usually pay a higher coupon than short-term bonds, and bonds from companies that may default have to pay higher premiums to attract investors than do, for example, bonds of agencies of the federal government.

Academic research shows that little is gained by holding bonds of long maturities. These are especially subject to the ill effects of inflation. That effect, called interest-rate risk, more than outweighs their higher coupons. Research also indicates that high-yield bonds (so-called junk bonds) do not typically reward their holders with extra income after their high default rates are taken into account.

If you have a family office managing a 50 million dollar fixed-income portfolio, you might want to consider purchasing individual bonds. Otherwise, you often will be better off in a no-load, low-expense, high-quality short-term bond mutual fund. The exception to this rule would be government securities, which you buy with no transaction costs straight from Uncle Sam at www.publicdebt.treas.gov/sec/sectrdir.htm. Scott Burns, the astute columnist for the *Dallas Morning News,* points out in his column of December 17, 2002 that a simple 5-year Treasury note outperforms government bond funds about 87 percent of the time.

Municipal bonds are in order for bonds that must be held in taxable accounts, at least for individuals above the lowest income tax brackets. Civic municipalities need money, and the yields on the bonds they issue have the attraction of being free of federal taxes, and usually state taxes as well in the states where they are issued. As of this writing, municipal bonds are yielding about 5 percent, compared to about 7 percent for high-grade corporate bonds.

The government issues Treasury Inflation-Protected Securities (TIPS). Historically, the biggest risk to fixed-income investment holders has been inflation, which destroys both the value of their bond's principal and interest. Inflation-protected securities hedge against this risk, and do so without taking a deduction in the event of deflation. The government simply adjusts your final return of principal by the Consumer Price Index. This effectively means that, unlike with other long-term bonds, there is no penalty for owning long-term TIPS. Currently only a few companies offer these in convenient bond funds, notably Vanguard, Fidelity, and Pimco, but more are coming. Since you have to pay tax on the undistributed annual income from these bonds, they are best kept in tax-free accounts.

There is a reason why Ian Fleming did not name Agent 007 "James Stock." We love bonds in a portfolio. It is very satisfying to receive cash payments that come in like clockwork.

What place should bonds occupy in your investment portfolio? Pension funds typically keep an allocation of 60 percent stocks/40 percent bonds for their long-term investors. Your mileage may vary. A percentage equal to your age is not a bad place to open the discussion. If you are 25, keep 25 percent of your portfolio in bonds; if you are 50, keep 50 percent of your portfolio in bonds. If you feel very strong and healthy, you might want less in bonds. Another answer is that of Benjamin Graham, who believed that a 50 percent stocks/50 percent bonds allocation was the proper default position, which could vary by as much as 25 percentage points in either direction depending on market conditions. When the stock market seems fully valued, Graham would have you tactically shifting more money to your bond position. When the market appears inexpensive, it is time to go shopping for stocks. When the 8 Ball says, "Ask Again Later," maintain the 50–50 defensive allocation.

If you buy a bond fund in a taxable account, make sure you don't buy it just before it is ready to make a distribution, or you will find a portion of your investment immediately handed back to you in taxable form. (The same holds true for stock funds, especially toward year's end.)

Stocks

Stocks are sometimes miraculous and sometimes a bag of snakes. They give your portfolio *mojo* power to grow when they perform well, which is most of the time, but they must be handled with extreme care to keep from biting you. That said, we do not recommend purchasing individual stocks. Unless you want to monitor a portfolio of 50 or so companies, you will be taking on something called *unsystematic risk.* This is a risk inherent in the fluctuation of individual stock prices that goes beyond the risk of participation in the stock market as a whole. A bag holds 100 black and 100 white marbles. You reach in and pull out five: four white and a black. Your sampling error has given you a skewed outcome. It may be lucky, or it may be unlucky. However, no one is underwriting your mistake if you guess wrong. Achieving this unusual outcome is unnecessary and you are not compensated for assuming it. It is better to hold all the marbles. The S&P's 500 Index includes 500 of the largest capitalization stocks in the United States—a winner's circle, in which new entrants are continuously crowding out the weak sisters that have fallen behind.

Even if you decide to gamble on a handful of stocks, you are unlikely to do better than the S&P 500 Index as a whole. Academic studies have repeatedly shown that most active managers underperform the market averages. All those smart-sounding people we hear on CNBC and *Wall Street Week*, with their expensive suits and terrific haircuts, with all their time and study and access to every sort of information—these clever folks repeatedly underperform the market averages. Since virtually everything that can be known about a stock is already built into its price, stock picking usually adds little value (in fact, it tends to add negative value). Meanwhile, the transaction costs of trading, taxes, bid-ask spreads, and management expenses erode your holdings.

This inability of active managers to consistently beat the S&P is actually of benefit to the ordinary investor. It means that the experts are constantly applying their skills to pricing the market, giving us a free ride. Imagine how much work it would be if you had to come up with a rational price for every stock all on your own. The prudent investor lets others do the heavy lifting and piggybacks on their effort. As Benjamin Franklin said, "Fools give feasts and wise men eat them." There is no other field where a total amateur can step onto the field and beat a pro. Chess? Tennis? Not a chance. You may enjoy shooting hoops on Saturday morning, you may even be pretty good at it, but step on to the court with Shaq and Kobe and they are going to mop up the arena with your hide. You may have a low handicap and routinely take money from your friends on the golf course, but if you play with Tiger Woods, you are going to get beat. Yet when you buy the entire S&P 500 Index, you not only compete with Shaq and Tiger as their full equal, you will beat them most of the time. This raises the question as to whether there is really any such thing as professional expertise when it comes to stock picking, but that is a subject for another day.

With so much money at stake, not to mention pride, the issue of active stock picking versus passive indexing arouses strong feelings, and readers interested in following the debate will enjoy Burton Malkiel's classic *A Random Walk Down Wall Street.*

However, there is an even more compelling reason why Market Timers following our philosophy should index.

The research in this book is based on the performance of the S&P 500 Index as recorded over the past century—including established scholarly reconstructions by Cowles for the pre-1926 period before the S&P 500 Index formally existed. When you buy the S&P 500 Index as a whole, you are coming as close as you can to reproducing the results we outline. It is a matter of repeatability.

Frankly, we have no idea how to go about timing the purchase or sale of individual stocks. If you choose to go this route, good luck and goodbye. Our interest is in helping the risk-averse, conservative investor, who more prudently chooses to buy the market as a whole.

Virtually everyone offers an S&P 500 Index fund these days. The grandfather is Vanguard's S&P 500 fund (ticker: VFINX), and similar funds are available at Fidelity (FSMKX), T. Rowe Price (PREIX), Schwab (SWPIX) and elsewhere, although sometimes with much higher fund expenses: Beware! If you have a brokerage account, you can buy S&P's Depositary Receipts, called Spiders (ticker: SPY) or iShares (IVV) just like any other stock.

There are tradeoffs between holding the index in a mutual fund like the Vanguard Index 500 or as a trust share like Spiders. You can buy the funds with no commission, which make them ideal for people who are making regular deposits. On the other hand, redeeming these shares can be cumbersome, and you can only buy and sell at the net asset value at the close of the day. Spiders or iShares can be bought and sold whenever the market is open, but you will have commissions to pay as well. Never pay a load for an S&P 500 Index fund.

One minor side-benefit of the recent general collapse of stock prices is that many of these funds (especially the newer ones) now carry negative capital gains liabilities. That is, any capital gains they accumulate going forward should be offset for years to come by losses they are carrying on their books.

That said, we do not endorse a hidebound S&P 500 only-ism. Putting a portion of your stock holdings into a foreign stock index fund, and a portion into a small capitalization stock index fund will variegate your equity returns. All these funds are widely available, although they may not reside on the limited bill of fare at your company's 401(k) plan. Since the S&P 500 is currently a large capitalization growth fund, investors may also wish to counterweight their portfolios with a low price-to-book "value" index fund as well, both domestically and abroad. These approaches are perfectly agreeable. We are also quite fond of Diamonds—not the kind that are a girl's best friend, but rather the unit investment trust (ticker: DIA) that tracks the Dow Jones Industrial Average. The research presented here, however, is tied to the S&P 500 Index.

If you need money to fund the purchase of a house in five years or a college education in 10 years, it is an open question to what extent stocks should play a role in your portfolio. While, at their best, they will dramatically outperform all other asset classes, it is also possible that you will lose a lot of money and a lot of sleep.

The supposedly wonderful compound return from U.S. stocks throughout the nineteenth century has been shown to suffer from *survivorship bias*. That is, these returns were calculated only using companies that were left standing at the end of the century, and fail to take account of all the canal stocks, mining stocks, small town bank stocks, and uncounted others that went out of business along the way. We cannot take comfort in a historical guarantee of equity outperformance.

If you bought the stock market in 1901, you were still in the red 20 years later. If you bought the market in the year 1906, by 1921 you still would have been down 16 percent—even after inflation and with all dividends reinvested. If you bought the market at the end of 1928, in 1942 you would have been down 19 percent after inflation and with all dividends reinvested (never mind all the taxes you would have had to pay en route). The investor who bought the market in 1972 was up less than 1 percent by 1984, but still in negative territory after taxes are taken into account. This is using the U.S. stock market as your benchmark, which is a bit like using the 1950s New York Yankees as your standard in baseball. Cubs' fans had a different experience. Maybe the United States will continue to bat ball after ball out of the stadium in the century ahead, but if regression to the mean counts for anything, there is every chance that the performance of our stock market may more closely approximate that of other countries' stock markets around the world. In *Triumph of the Optimists,* Dimson, Marsh, and Staunton conclude their academic survey of 101 years of global investing with the disturbing forecast that stocks have significant probabilities (17 percent to 23 percent) of underperforming the risk-free T-bill rate for even 40- or 50-year holding periods. If the prospect of getting these kinds of returns does not concern you, perhaps you have not thought about it seriously enough.

It is said that for $100 in savings to become $110 is a miracle, while for $100,000,000 to become $110,000,000 is almost inevitable. The cruel paradox is that those individuals who most need the boost from equity returns are typically the ones who can least afford to lose the money, while multimillionaires, pension funds, and foundations can enjoy the excess returns from socking money away for decades without touching it. We have just come off a period of enormous excess equity valuation. Is it really possible that in 2011, your stocks still will be worth less than they were in 2000?

Absolutely. Prices have gotten so far ahead of earnings that it might well take 10 years for earnings to catch up and restore price/earnings ratios to normal. In the meantime, you might have done better with cash or bonds or real estate. Stocks typically have gone up a real 6.7 percent per year, but not when they start as high as they were in 2000.

Although we preach diversification, we do not recommend that you invest in commodities like orange juice futures or collectibles like vintage Fender Stratocasters unless you are a full-time dealer who profits from other people's enthusiasm for them.

Being highly diversified, your total returns every year will not track the S&P 500 or any published index. If the Nasdaq goes to 5000, your holdings will not. If the Nasdaq goes to 200, your holdings will not. It always will be possible to track any subcomponent of your portfolio against an index, but if you have indexed everything to begin with, there is not much reason to bother. It may be that your stock portfolio lost money, but what happened to the value of homes on your street?

Asset Allocation

Managing money is about the unglamorous task of being a defensive lineman, not the star quarterback. You have to make some ongoing decisions about the ratio between your holdings in the four asset categories we have mentioned, including where to put any new monies that become available. This is the practice of *asset allocation.*

Portfolio managers make a big deal about this. In 1990, Harry Markowitz won the Nobel Prize in economics for his insight that an optimal portfolio can be constructed for any given level of investment risk you choose to take. Money managers hold this esoteric knowledge over our heads as if it were the secret formula for Orange Julius. Armed with their means-variance optimizers, they confidently plot out exactly how we should distribute our money among investment classes to as many decimal places as we could want.

There is only one problem. The inputs required for their analyzes are unknown and, alas, unknowable. No one knows the future returns from equities, or bonds, or any asset class. No one knows the future variability of these returns, or what their correlations will be. This means that all these statistically derived

portfolio allocations, while incredibly precise, are just preten-
tiously dressed up hunches. As William Bernstein pointed out,
for the period from 1977 to 1996, the best asset combination to
hold was an equally weighted portfolio of U.S. Small Cap, Japa-
nese, and Precious Metal stocks. This combination beat the S&P
500 Index by an impressive 3 percent on an annualized basis.
Does this have any bearing on how we should invest today? None
whatever.

Yet if we do not plug in the historical data, what inputs
should we use? If we really knew what asset class was going to go
up the most, there would be no need for asset allocation at all—
we would just bet on the winning horse.

Another answer is that we should allocate our investments to
mirror that of the market as a whole. Yet how many investment
advisors recommend putting more than 50 percent of our assets
in foreign stocks and bonds to reflect the reality of the global
market? Or putting 20 percent of our assets in Japan? Even the
most ardent efficient marketers back away from this cliff.

Despite what financial professionals would like you to believe, there is no *a priori* right answer for asset allocation. This
emperor has no clothes. The price, price/earnings multiple, price-
to-dividends ratio, price-to-book ratio, price-to-sales ratio, price-
to-cash flow ratio, and stock versus bond yields all point to the
general direction for stocks ahead, but only over long periods of
time and with no precision at all year-to-year.

Portfolio Rebalancing

If there is no such thing as a perfect asset allocation, it is difficult
to see the point of constantly retuning the portfolio to some
Pythagorean proportion. Financial planners who claim to shun
market timing like a festering sore are forever recommending that
clients annually rebalance their portfolios. But what is rebalancing

except—closet Market Timing? Rebalancing is nothing more than selling assets which have disproportionately increased in value (sell high) to buy assets that have not kept up (buy low).

The problem is that these short-term fluctuations may be based on nothing more than the short-term vagaries of the market. It is not that they are doing crypto Market Timing that is the problem, but that they are doing it in an unprincipled way—typically using a one-year average as the benchmark, which is too short. Consider the year 2001. Stocks are down 12 percent, bonds are up 8 percent. Does this mean that you should sell your bonds to top off your stocks? Yes, says your financial planner, committed to the ritual of rebalancing. This is a terrible idea. The price/earnings ratio of the S&P 500 Index was over 40 at year's end. Stocks were still overpriced.

It gets worse.

Imagine that two people each put $500 in stocks and $500 in bonds at the end of 1901. One lets his accounts run wild throughout the century, while the other sedulously rebalances his stock and bond accounts at the end of each year, selling whichever account is higher and using the proceeds to make up the difference for the account that lags behind. If his stocks are worth $600 and his bonds are worth $400 at the end of the year, he sells $100 worth of stocks and buys bonds so that both accounts are worth $500 once more. Did we mention that this triggers capital gains taxes as well?

One hundred years later, at the end of 2001, the person who let his accounts run wild would have a total of $243,727, while the constant rebalancer would have just $83,001 (less all the taxes he has paid en route).

What accounts for this enormous difference? As we keep mentioning, the twentieth century was a good time for stocks, but a bad one for bonds (because of inflation, the bond's mortal enemy). Fully $241,354 of the $243,727 in the wild man's total returns has come from stocks, while his $500 bond position has appreciated to only $2,373. Selling stocks to pour them into bonds every year would have completely derailed the total returns of this long-term investor.

With one important consequence: The rebalancer's portfolio is still balanced 50/50 in the end, same as when he started. That is some consolation, anyway. The investor who let his portfolio run wild has watched his asset allocation shift from 50 percent stocks/50 percent bonds in 1902 to 99 percent stocks/1 percent bonds at the start of 2002. This is not a prudent ratio for someone whose great grandchildren must be nearing retirement by now.

What should you do if, because of the tremendous success of one asset class or failure of another, your holdings become so lopsided that they are no longer diversified? If you are going to adjust your asset allocation, what should guide you?

Answer: The valuation of the stock market, of course.

Reallocate your portfolio, if necessary, but do so by buying stocks when they are cheap, or by selling them to buy more bonds when stocks are expensive.

Consider once more the case of two investors who are husbanding a portfolio through the past century. Both of them started out 1901 with an allocation of $500 in the S&P 500 Index and $500 in 10-year Treasury bonds. Both prudently decide to readjust their stock/bond allocation whenever it gets out of alignment by making small (5 percent) moves from one asset class to the other when the occasion demands. However, one of them is a Market Timer, and using our timing signals, he waits for a time when stocks are fully valued to sell them, and waits until they are undervalued to buy more.

Figure 8.1 shows the results of 100 years of portfolio management and re-allocation according to these guidelines, allowing for different degrees of deviation from a 50/50 stock/bond portfolio. Note how the larger the tracking error (the variance from the 50/50 stock/bond allocation) they tolerated, the bigger the pot is in the end. While we all want to do what we can to improve our investment performance, here it pays to not be

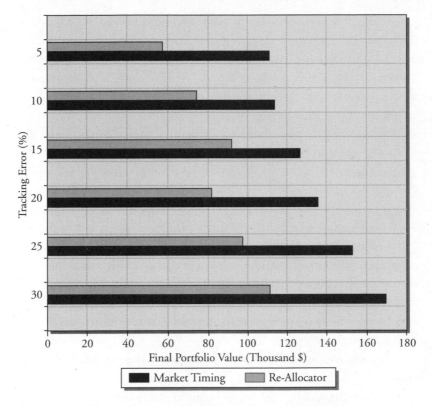

Figure 8.1   Asset Reallocation, 1902–2001

obsessive. This freedom also gives the Market Timer plenty of time to pick his buying and selling opportunities, and this led, on average, to his having 55 percent more money at the end of the century than his Non-Market Timing cohort, across all degrees of portfolio tracking error.

Timing Costs

What about the penalty the Market Timer pays for being out of the market when an upswing hits?

Every few months, the Sunday supplement carries an article with the dire warning that if you missed the 90 best days from 1963 to 1993, your investment performance would have dropped from 11.8 percent annually to a scant 3.3 percent. The implication is clear: start playing footsie with the stock market and your returns are going to crater.

What these articles fail to mention is that if you missed the 90 worst days in the market over that same period, your returns would skyrocket from 11.8 percent to 23.6 percent. Once again, the double-edged sword of reason cuts both ways. By the way, didn't most of those 90 best days occur when the market was low? And didn't most of the 90 worst days happen when it was high?

There can be long periods when there are no buy signals whatever. If you came into an inheritance in 1988, no signal presented here would have suggested that you buy until 1995 (looking at the monthly, not annual, data). During this time, the total return on stocks was 16 percent better than the return on bonds, and had you been out of the market, you would have missed it.

The timing signals also would have kept you out of the market during the heady period from 1925 through 1931. Not a problem there, though: during this period, stocks went up 4 percent, compared to a 22 percent increase in government bonds.

If you started out investing in 1955 using this method, you would not have found a buying opportunity until 1965. During this time, you would have missed a short-term stock upswing of 236 percent, while holding bonds that only increased in value by 32 percent. Although the 20-year returns from buying 1955 through 1964 were poor, it would have been difficult to watch the Huntley-Brinkley news hour many nights and see the glowing stock market returns while you sat on the sidelines.

One could argue that this is the price you pay for having some insurance you were not overpaying at other times, such as by keeping you out of the market in 1929 and 1999.

Here, as always, diversification becomes relevant. One should always strive to have holdings in each major asset class, even at the risk of overpaying. Someone starting out investing in 1955 should have held some stocks.

Note that we have limited our search to annual and monthly data. It is possible that someone who followed the stock market more closely might have found some daily or even intraday occasion to invest when prices were more to his liking, given the market's volatility.

In the end, the opportunity costs of market timing have not been prohibitive, even during a sensational century for stocks and an abysmal one for fixed income investing. The dollar cost averaging Market Timers referred to in each chapter incur all opportunity costs, and they still manage to beat the Non-Market Timers by 3.9 percent annually over the past 100 years and 3.5 percent annually over the past 25 years.

There is another answer to the question of opportunity costs. It goes like the old joke: What do you do when you move to a new town where the dating partners don't come up to your standards?

Answer: Lower your standards.

We can do the same thing with our Market Timing signals. Not all months or years are equally bad. If we buy into a year where the market is priced "Above Average," we will still do significantly better in the long run that buying a year when it is priced "High." The investor starting out in the mid-1950s might have chosen to add to his position in 1957, when the market moved to within a few percentage points of his buy sign. The idea is not to achieve some Platonic portfolio perfectionism, it is to avoid overpaying for stocks given the constraints of the real-world investing environment.

After three terrible years, as of late 2002, the S&P 500 finally has been bludgeoned into an attractive valuation range. Even before now, however, not all the major stock indices were equally overvalued. Earlier in 2002, the Dow was selling at a price/earnings multiple in the mid-twenties (high but not insane), compared to the S&P 500's price/earnings multiple of 39 and the Nasdaq at a price/earnings ratio that is noncomputable because the total earnings for all Nasdaq companies is a negative number. A person beginning to invest then might have nibbled at some Diamonds (the unit trust shares for the Dow Jones Industrial Average sold on the American Stock Exchange) rather than Spiders (the proxy for the S&P 500) or QQQs (the proxy for the Nasdaq 100).

There are also other investments besides large stocks. The general principle we have been espousing is that an investment may be a bargain when its current price is lower than its long-term price. For example, Figure 8.2 shows the results of dollar cost averaging into 90-day Treasury bills during the past 50 years, while in Figure 8.3 we do the same with 10-year government bonds during the entire past century. Both charts contrast the total real returns secured by buying each of these instruments when the yield they offered was either above or below their 15-year moving averages. The answer in both cases is to buy when their yield is high.

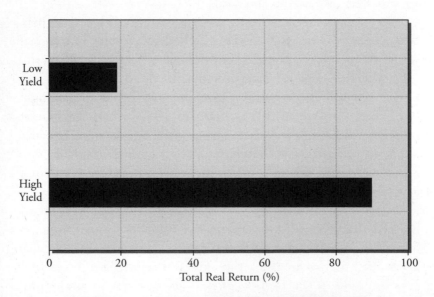

Figure 8.2   Total Real Returns from T-Bills Bought above or below Average Yield, 1950–2000

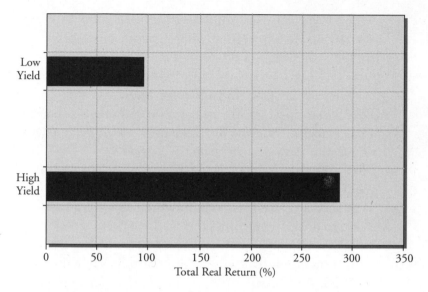

Figure 8.3   Total Real Returns from Treasury Bonds Bought above or below 15-Year Average, 1902–2001

In recent years, new indices have sprouted up that keep track of foreign stocks, small capitalization stocks, growth stocks, value stocks, and real estate investment trusts. The indices being new, we have no data as yet to back up this contention, yet we shall not be surprised to discover that buying low proves a good strategy in these markets as well, since it works in every other market of which we are aware.

With this in mind, it may be instructive to revisit the period from 1988 to 1994, and again from 1996 to 2001, when stocks were out of favor by these long-term valuation criteria, and see whether any alternative investments might have commended themselves to our attention:

- In 1988, with mortgage rates hovering at 10.7 percent, this might have been a good year to pay down your mortgage. This is equivalent to buying a completely risk-free bond with a yield equal to your mortgage rate, and with zero transaction costs or account maintenance expenses.

- In 1989, the yield on 90-day Treasury bills (8.27 percent) was now higher than its long-term average. This would have been a safe place to park some money.
- For 1990 to 1994, mortgage rates were still higher than the yield available from the bond market, which made paying down your mortgage an attractive option.
- For 1996, the National Association of Real Estate Investment Trusts reports that prices of Real Estate Investment Trusts (REITs) have fallen below their long-term average. Time to diversify into REITS?
- In 1997, mortgage rates continued to be higher than the yield from bonds. Everything else was fully valued.
- In 1998, the Russell 2000 Index of small companies fell below its long-term average. Small company stocks behave differently from the large company stocks that are found in the S&P 500 Index, and even outperform them over long periods of time. This was likely a good time to diversify into this asset class.
- Both buying REITs and paying down mortgages continue to be viable options during what was clearly a stock market bubble in 1999.
- In 2000, as the stock market crumpled, yields on T-bills (6.17 percent) rose above their long-term norm. A safe port in a storm.
- In 2001, small cap stock valuations stood out once more.
- In 2002, the S&P 500 Index was down fully 49 percent from its peak, and the Morgan Stanley EAFE index of foreign stocks dipped below its 15-year moving average for the first time. The Russell 2000 index of small cap stocks was also priced low relative to its long-term trend.

Undoubtedly, others would have been led to draw different conclusions, even by the same data. Our point is to show the kind of judgment calls that a price-sensitive investor might have to make during times when S&P 500 prices are high. Since the true value of the stock market can take years to become apparent, we do not yet know the relative wisdom of all these roads not taken. Perhaps they would have been dead ends. Certainly they would have led to a more diversified and conservative set of holdings than those held by some of our friends, who jumped with both feet into Telecom and the Internet, became instantly rich, and then lost everything.

Opportunity costs are greatest, and the advantage to a buy and hold strategy most pronounced, when a bull market carries on for a prolonged period, and when the returns from stocks are significantly better than those from bonds and T-bills. Both conditions held for much of the past century, yet in spite of this, surprisingly, Market Timing still added value. When the market is fluctuating, and when the returns from stocks are not significantly greater than those from fixed-income investments—perhaps a time such as we face now—then Market Timing comes into its own.

What if the coming century turns out to be an unmitigated disaster for stocks? A Bizarro twentieth-century graph turned upside down? Buy-and-hold approaches will suffer the most, but Market Timing won't offer any ultimate protection either, as the plunging stock price will be forever below its long-term averages, signaling buy even as the Titanic sinks.

Which leads us to our fourth piece of advice.

4. PROCEED WITH CAUTION

Across an investment lifetime, it is far more important that you avoid doing something really stupid than that you should do something astoundingly brilliant. To put it another way, the brilliant investor is the one who avoids stupid, preventable mistakes. Remember: You don't have to be stupid to do something dumb with your money. Lots of really smart people do dumb things with their money every day. Wall Street will teach you humility and respect for powers beyond your control. That is a promise.

Herewith a few basic thoughts that have proved useful over time:

- Never make a "bold" investment decision.
- Don't think big.
- Don't make any sudden moves.
- Never move more than a small percentage of your money around in any one day or transaction (except for the day you buy your house).
- Do not put off the day when you finally understand and take charge of your finances.
- Have you noticed that you can lose a fortune investing in Morningstar Five-Star funds?
- Do not invest in things you do not understand; do not put a penny in a gumball machine unless you can see a gumball inside the machine.
- Speaking of pennies, do not invest in "penny" stocks.
- Do not pay high sales loads, fees, and commissions.
- Do not assume that anyone you see on television or read in the paper who is giving investment advice has the slightest idea what he is talking about, including us. Believe what data say is believable.
- Ignore all stock tips and ignore everything your neighbor says, even if he drives a Mercedes.
- The financial media are starved for content and so will give a platform to anyone. Pay no attention to analysts, fund managers, or the latest whiz kids.
- When you come to the inevitable lists of the best performing stocks and mutual funds, turn the page . . . invariably. Last quarter's data is meaningless. Remember our discussion of regression to the mean? How what goes up comes down?

- Charlatans are everywhere, and if you have money to invest, they will find you.
- Are you by chance wealthy? A "high net worth" individual? That special handling everyone is giving you is merely the anesthetic that precedes the surgical removal of your wallet. When done skillfully, you will hardly notice the missing money for months or years.
- Always be aware of the financial motives and conflicts of interest of anyone who wants to get within a mile of your money, no matter how friendly and confident and well connected he or she seems.
- Do not even think of doing anything the IRS might legitimately question. Overpay your taxes rather than risk having G-Men come to your house at 4:00 A.M., haul you to jail, and seize all your assets.
- Never accept any unsolicited financial advice or take cold calls from brokers.
- Do not invest a large part of your 401(k) in your company stock or even in the same industry if you can help it. If hard times hit your company, you may be out of a job and simultaneously find your portfolio diminished (and if you live in a company town, the value of your home may be adversely affected as well).
- Do not invest in a store because you see a lot of customers there at the mall or because you like the coffee or blue jeans or jelly beans. Sales do not equal profits.
- If someone wants to sell you an annuity, consider it carefully for several years. Notice how eager they are for you to sign? Their commission will be large, while the possibility that it is really an appropriate investment vehicle for you can be small.
- If you have a spectacular idea that will require most or all of your capital to start but promises to make you a multimillionaire within five years, call us up and for a mere 10

percent of your money we will be glad to talk you out of it. It will be the smartest phone call you ever made.

- Take a long walk through the park before tying up your money in illiquid investments. That money you do not need for five years? What if you need it next week?
- Does the word *synergy* appear in the prospectus? *Black box? Vertical Integration? Paradigm? Chaos Theory?* Run!
- Check your driver's license. Is your last name Spielberg? If not, do not invest in a motion picture limited partnership. In Hollywood, there is a name for people who take a serious interest in film and who secretly entertain the thought of going into the motion picture business one day. They are called *the public.* Hollywood accounting makes certain you will never see a dime.
- Before making an investment, try explaining the rationale to your wife. Does she look at you the way Alice Cramden looks at Ralph on *The Honeymooners* when he is describing his latest get-rich-quick scheme? That look may be telling you something.
- Finally, do not use this book in ways it was not intended. Our endorsement of classic valuation measures to price and therefore time the stock market does not mean that we stand behind every crackpot with a mimeograph machine selling a Market Timing newsletter. Do not assume you can make money by shorting the market whenever our timing signals say the market is high. Do not switch willy nilly from 100 percent stocks to 100 percent bonds or cash whenever a timing shift occurs. If the stock market were predictable to this extent, it would not be the stock market as we know and love it.

We hope to have shown you how being aware of the value of stocks when you buy and sell can thereby increase your total return. Perhaps you would care to know where the stock market stands today by these valuation criteria. Is right now a good time to buy? As we have mentioned, *Barron's* publishes many of the figures you need, and the articles by Tom Donlan and Alan Abelson are always worth reading. Many of the numbers are also available in the *Wall Street Journal, Investors Business Daily,* the business section of the Sunday *New York Times,* your local newspaper, as well as various places online if you care to Google them up.

Or, you can go straight to our Web site:

www.yesyoucantimethemarket.com

and find them right now. For free.

Chapter Nine

Looking Forward:
A Note of Caution

There are good reasons why the general party line from brokers and investment gurus is that Market Timing does not work. Those reasons are closely connected to the reasons why market timing can and does in fact work—or at least has worked in the distant and recent past. They have to do with what stocks are, what attitudes are, and with decisions about when to start and stop the clock.

Start with why it looks in many cases as if stock market timing does not work. For most of the last hundred years, stocks were chronically underpriced. For reasons having to do with perceived risk, economic cycles, and mass psychology, investors over a very long period often would not pay as much for stocks as they were worth (again, as always, we are referring to stocks as a group, not to individual stock choice). There were reasons for the typically low price of stocks. Stocks were and are volatile. Volatility, especially downward volatility, is frightening. Once burned, investors are twice shy. Stocks are the lowest and last on the food chain when a company goes into bankruptcy or another form of reorganization compelled by financial straits. They have the last claim on whatever corporate assets are left after paying creditors. Volatility plus low claims on assets can and did depress prices.

While stocks had higher yields in terms of dividends than bonds did in terms of coupons for most of the century just past, those dividends were variable and could be altered or passed. This, too, made stocks seem less desirable than they often were.

Thus, stocks had weighing on their price what has come to be known as the *equity risk premium.* This was a premium that issuers had to pay or a discount that buyers got to accept for the fluctuating fortunes of stocks, their variable dividends, and their late claim on assets in receivership.

For most of the twentieth century, equity risk premium was simply too high. That is, stocks were priced too low, and thus buying them yielded excellent returns. For decades after the Great Depression especially, the prices of stocks reflected a genuine terror that stocks would collapse again as they did in the 1929–1933 period and in 1937. If an investor bought them with that shadow still on them, he tended to do well, just as buying any asset when it is low tends to give better returns than buying when it is high. (That's what this book is all about.)

On a more basic level, or what economists would call a macro level, stocks reflect corporate earnings. They are basically a way to capture corporate earnings for the investor. The fall in corporate earnings was so enormous in the 1929–1933 period (Figure 9.1) that investors were spooked for decades afterward that such a thing could happen again. This fear of a possible recurrence of a Great Depression also bore down on stock prices, keeping them low.

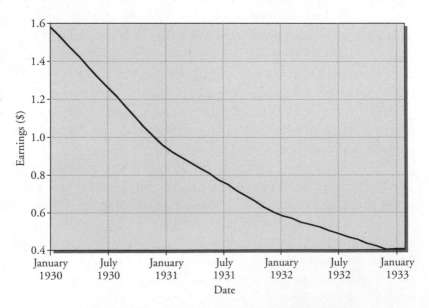

Figure 9.1   Corporate Earnings, 1929–1933

Thus, buyers who bought in the period after 1933 bought when stocks were insanely low in retrospect, and enjoyed immense gains as the decades wore on and as investors came to believe there would not be another Great Depression, another collapse in corporate profits . . . and took the equity risk premium (or discount depending on which end you are looking at) out of stock prices.

A look at stock prices after the vast collapse of 1929–1933 until early 2000 (Figure 9.2) shows an impressively angled line trending upward with a few very temporary but occasionally very sharp dips.

Betting that you would do better to time the market than to bet in favor of this immense bull run of some six and a half decades was often wrong. In a way, the situation is analogous to someone at a casino roulette table who is betting half of the time on red and half of the time on black. But unknown to him, the wheel will only allow the ball to land on the red. His fortunes will

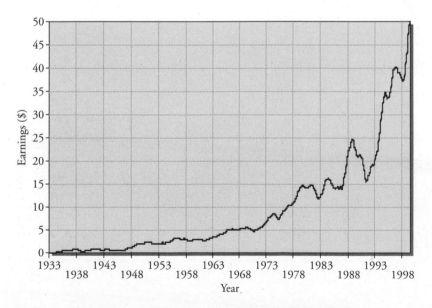

Figure 9.2   Corporate Earnings, 1933–2000

be poor. Similarly, the after-effects of the Great Depression and the great stock collapse of the same period virtually compelled stocks to be underpriced for a long time—and thus to offer buying opportunities in most years. It seemed as if it were just plain foolish to bet against what seemed like a perpetual bull move.

To be sure, there were blips such as the 1937 recession, the tech booms and busts of the late 1960s and early 1970s, and worst of all, the calamitous recessionary inflation (or inflationary recession) of the mid-1970s. In these periods, the equity risk premium had come off and then came on again in a great hurry, or else earnings had to be compared with ultra high bond yields and thus seemed low. Inflation in the mid- and late-1970s also raised the interest rate at which corporate earnings were discounted back to the present. This caused an immense fall in the present value of future earnings—just as the fall in interest rates through most of the 1990s caused a large rise in the present value of future earnings. (Inflation depresses stock prices for a variety of other reasons, too, including the difficulty of maintaining adequate reserves for true

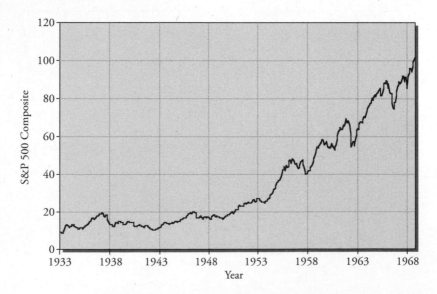

Figure 9.3   S&P 500, 1933–1968

depreciation, but the impossibility of competing with very high bond yields and the cost of discounting earnings to present value are the basics.)

Again, however, over very long periods, it did indeed seem as if betting against the market was a fool's errand, and as if betting that you could tell when the market was going to do less well than in other years was a virtual impossibility.

Part of the fallacy in that approach had to do with choosing what time periods you would work with.

That is, there was always the extreme problem of deciding in which years you were going to begin and end your comparisons. If you started with 1933 and went up to 1968 (Figure 9.3), it sure looked as if anyone but a moron would just buy and hold.

If you started with 1982 and went up until February of 2000 (Figure 9.4), again, you looked very foolish trying to time the market or even doing anything but buying and holding.

But if you took a different tack, and different beginning and ending points, you got very different results. Again, stock prices

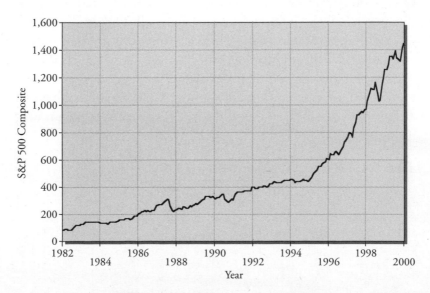

Figure 9.4   S&P 500, 1982–2000

are a proxy for corporate earnings and blended in are expectations of future earnings, always discounted by expectations of inflation as reflected in interest rates. In the period from 1929 to 1933, as corporate earnings collapsed during a period of worldwide serious monetary mismanagement, stock prices came down with them.

The investor who had said that fundamentals looked very pricey in this period, that earnings could not possibly rise enough to justify them, and had sold then would have looked brilliant (Table 9.1). You would have to be a fool to do anything but attempt to market time, bet on the reversion to a lower number . . . and take your cash off the table. Then, buy and hold looked idiotic, not market timing.

Similarly, during the 1960s (Table 9.2), you would also conclude that you would have been insane not to have at least tried to time the market.

If 1974 were the year you had to sell all of your stocks to pay for a catastrophic illness, you would indeed have wished you had timed the market and gone to cash before the 1970s inflationary crash. You would have seen corporate profits adjusted for inflation and relative to interest rates take a big fall. That is, if you take certain time horizons, you get good results from market timing and poor results from buy and hold.

Indeed, this can be true for extremely long periods. The stock market did not reach its level of summer 1929 for almost 25 years afterward. The stock market did not permanently cross intraday

Table 9.1   Market Valuations, 1926–1930

Year	Price	P/E	Dividends	Tobin's Q	20 Years Later (%)
1926	Above Average	Below Average	High	Above Average	147
1927	High	High	High	High	72
1928	High	High	High	High	19
1929	High	Above Average	High	High	58
1930	High	High	Above Average	Above Average	143

Table 9.2   Market Valuations, 1960–1968

Year	Price	P/E	Dividends	Tobin's Q	20 Years Later (%)
1960	High	High	High	High	71
1961	High	High	High	High	18
1962	High	High	High	High	54
1963	High	High	High	High	50
1964	High	High	High	High	33
1965	High	Above Average	High	High	53
1966	High	Below Average	Above Average	Above Average	107
1967	High	Above Average	High	High	73
1968	High	Above Average	Above Average	High	83

highs of 1966 for close to 15 years. Adjusted for inflation, the stock market as measured by the Dow did not reach 1929 levels for close to 65 years. (However, because dividend yields were so high during much of that time, your returns would have been far better than the raw numbers of the Dow say.) And this was the Dow Jones Industrial Average—not the Nasdaq.

Again, however, if you start your timing in 1933, and go for about 40 years afterward, almost any time horizon after 1969 gives you a big gain and makes Market Timing look futile.

Or, if you have a perpetual time horizon, that is, are immortal, you might well simply forget about Market Timing. (Of course, if you are immortal, you lose many of the fears and concerns that mortals have.) Over periods of a century or so, stocks have looked extremely good. This may explain in part why university endowments, typically entities with virtually perpetual time horizons, are not enthusiastic about Market Timing.

However, most of us do have time horizons. We cannot just blithely say, "Oh, we'll let time take care of that market collapse." Time certainly makes changes, but not necessarily changes that can be called progress toward solving anyone's special problems on any specific schedule. It is a myth, as Dr. Martin Luther King Jr.

wrote from Birmingham jail in 1963, to believe that ". . . progress rolls in on wheels of inevitability. . . ."

Here lies the rub. If you choose as your time horizon from
right now to when you will need the money, and if that period is
less than a two or three decades, Market Timing may not just be
interesting but compulsory. Even if U.S. stocks continue their winning streak and return 10 percent on average going forward, there
is no guarantee that an investor today will realize this return over
his or her investment lifetime. An investor who bought the Dow in
1929 had to wait 69 years to see that average 10 percent return,
even with dividends reinvested. You cannot just plunk your money
into the stock market reassured by the long-term historical average
and lie back in the hammock. You may not live to see it.

As investment advisor Steven Evanson correctly points out, an
investor who bought the S&P 500 in 1929 and waited 20 years
would have seen a real total return of 84 percent. Had he waited
until 1931 to invest, it would have been 818 percent. For a retiree,
that is the difference between eating hot dogs and filet mignon.

To look at it another way: The severe concern of the authors
is that the immense stock market boom of the late 1990s and
early 2000 caused a distortion in stocks as great as any that has
been witnessed so far and has given efforts to Market Time ur-
gency. The possibility is real that just as stocks were severely underpriced for a very long time after the Great Depression, the
stock market as a group may be persistently overpriced going forward. This might not be true of certain sectors, especially what
might be called "old line" industrial companies, but it might be
true of the S&P as a group and certainly of the Nasdaq as a
group. (The authors will be fascinated to see if the Nasdaq even
exists as a separate market 20 years from now.)

Here was the problem and here is the problem: Stocks reached
such an unheard of (literally unheard of, never before seen) level
in 1998, 1999, and 2000 that there simply were no metrics in financial history as precedent. If corporate earnings were to rise to

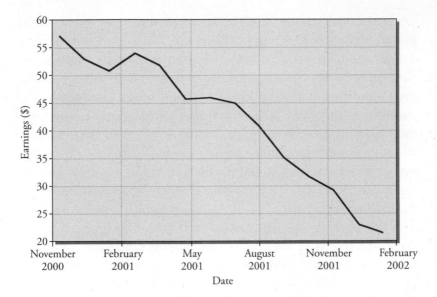

Figure 9.5   Corporate Earnings, 2000–2002

levels that rationalized such prices, they would have to skyrocket at an unprecedented level. As we all now know, they didn't rise at all. They fell (Figure 9.5). As a Dow measurement, an S&P measurement, or a national income accounts measurement, corporate profits have fallen spectacularly.

That means it would have been a smart thing to market time in the late 1990s (Table 9.3).

Table 9.3   Market Valuations, 1996–2000

Year	Price	P/E	Dividends	Tobin's Q
1996	High	High	High	High
1997	High	High	High	High
1998	High	High	High	High
1999	High	High	High	High
2000	High	High	High	High

Had investors looked at the price/earnings ratios, close to 50 for the S&P, close to 40 for the Dow, and said, "Holy Moses, these are just too high," and gone to cash, they would have been about the happiest campers in town. (The only happier ones would have been those who sold short.) If you took a look at the market and corporate profits and book values and asked yourself how these metrics stood up to historic levels, even to historic levels in boom times, you would have sold—and you would be well off. (Remember what Warren Buffett said about how the first rule of making money is not to lose money? And the second rule is to remember the first rule?)

If you had considered Market Timing as it is suggested in this book in 1999 and found that the market's position then was vastly above the 15-year moving average in terms of price/earnings ratios, price-to-book ratios, price/dividend ratios, or simple moving averages of price itself, you might have sold. You might at least have diversified and not poured gasoline onto the fire.

But our point is more troubling than that. Our point is that for a number of measurements, prices are still fantastically high. The *equity risk premium* has come off stocks with a vengeance still, even after the crash of 2000–2002. Because of excess optimism, or "irrational exuberance," or animal spirits, or just plain old ignorance, while earnings fell dramatically, proving vividly that there should indeed be a major risk premium in stocks, stock prices did not fall anywhere near as far or as fast.

In the height of the bubble, in early 2000, the S&P 500 was trading at close to 40 times earnings. That was and is a staggeringly frightening price. Now, as this book is being written, with clear evidence that stocks are indeed risky, the S&P 500 Index price/earnings ratio is still over 30. This is suggestive that investors have not fully digested just how risky stocks are. True, the Dow has fallen from levels of price/earnings near 30 to levels close to 20, levels that make at least some sense, but levels above 20 for the Dow are still extremely high by any historical measurement.

Our research tells us that if an investor buys stocks when their valuation levels are two or three standard deviations above average, there is no history of consistently making money from that starting point. Indeed, if an investor buys when stocks as measured by the Dow are above 25 as a price/earnings ratio, and carries out the series as long as it can be carried out until 2003, there is also no history of making money except in random spurts. Yale's Robert Shiller examined the periods following such price/earnings peaks and found that 20 years later, after inflation, your average annual return was likely to be in the −2 percent to 1.9 percent range. Plug these returns into your retirement calculator, and your jaw will drop.

If you go back to more typical price/earnings levels, the lesson is stark: Your likelihood of making money is an inverse function of the height of the price/earnings ratio in the year you started buying, of the price to book in the year you started buying, the price to dividend ratio in the year you started buying, the relative level of the price to the 15-year moving average or any of the measures we have used in this book. If you buy cheap by historic standards, your likelihood of making money is simply astronomically better than if you buy when stocks are dear by historic measurements.

And right now, stocks are still costly by historic standards. It may be that history is about to change, or it may not be. If it isn't, there are big problems ahead for those who bought high expecting big returns any time soon.

Or, maybe it makes sense to look at all of investing history that is available to us and note that while Market Timing may not work in the future, it certainly did work in the past, even in one of the most bullish centuries imaginable when buy-and-hold seemed unassailable. What is past is prologue, says a sign in front of the National Archives in Washington, DC. As we begin the twenty-first century, it might be good to remember this wisdom in stocks as in everything else in life.

Appendix

DATA SOURCES

You might think that with the Internet still in operation, reliable stock market data are as easy to get as today's weather. This is not our experience. While sales literature is easier than ever to obtain, finding the raw numbers and data series required to write this book took a bit of digging.

Here are some useful sources:

- www.globalfindata.com carries data series on the S&P 500 and other assets, including historical total returns from stocks and bonds if you don't care to calculate them yourselves.
- www.economy.com has historical data on the S&P, p/e ratios, dividends, interest rates, inflation, bond yields, and much else.
- www.econ.bbk.ac.uk/faculty/wright contains Professor Stephen Wright's data series on Tobin's Q as well as links to his excellent books and articles.
- aida.econ.yale.edu/~shiller/data.htm takes you to the Web site of Professor Robert Shiller, including his bone-chilling data on historical price/earnings ratios.
- www.barra.com/research/fundamentals.asp offers historical data on price-to-sales, price-to-cash flow, price-to-book, and a number of other measures.

DATA ANALYSIS

All attempts to extrapolate from a finite time period are susceptible to the charge of data mining. Perhaps we are seeing patterns based on a small sample that do not really apply elsewhere. One hundred years of stock market data certainly has its limitations. The past two centuries have been spectacular ones for America, yet civilizations decline as well as rise. Future research should focus on testing these findings using foreign markets and other time periods (although the quality of the data becomes suspect the further back we go), as well as indices besides the S&P 500.

Data mining becomes of particular concern where researchers start out with a large number of hypotheses that are tested, found wanting, and discarded while showcasing only those few surviving factors with predictive ability. This was not the case here. The only factors we examined are the ones presented.

It is important to note that our data are in no sense optimized. We have not tweaked our findings. For example, the time lines for comparing long-term versus current values could be adjusted until we found the crossover period that worked best for each factor. Then we could adjust the precise cutoff scores for each criterion so that it yielded the most discriminating buy signal. We could carefully select historical starting and ending points to showcase each factor to its best advantage. By cooking the books this way, we could have given the illusion of a far stronger case for our thesis that price-sensitive Market Timing adds utility. Instead, we have chosen a fixed long-term period (the 15-year moving average) for comparison for all factors, a fixed signaling point (crossing the mean), and fixed time periods (the past 100 and 25 years, as well as all rolling 5-, 10-, 15-, and 20-year subperiods). We hope these vanilla results prove rewarding for investors hoping to replicate them in the future.

Bibliography

Arnott, Robert, and Cliff Asness. "Does Dividend Policy Foretell Earnings Growth?" *Financial Analysts Journal* (2003).

Basu, Sanjoy. "Investment Performance of Common Stocks." *Journal of Finance* (June 1977).

Bernstein, William. *The Four Pillars of Investing.* New York: McGraw-Hill, 2001.

Bernstein, William. *The Intelligent Asset Allocator.* New York: McGraw-Hill, 2002.

Bogle, John. *Common Sense on Mutual Funds.* New York: John Wiley & Sons, 2000.

DeBondt, Werner, and Richard Thaler. "Does the Stock Market Overreact?" *Journal of Finance* (July, 1985).

Dimson, Elroy, Paul Marsh, and Mike Staunton. *Triumph of the Optimists.* Princeton, NJ: Princeton University Press, 2002.

Ellis, Charles, and John Brennan. *Winning the Loser's Game* 4th ed. New York: McGraw-Hill, 2002.

Graham, Benjamin. *The Intelligent Investor.* New York: Harper & Row, 1973.

Ibbotson, Roger. "Portfolios of the New York Stock Exchange," Working Paper. New Haven, CT: Yale School of Management, 1986.

Keppler, Michael. "Importance of Dividend Yield in Country Selection." *Journal of Portfolio Management,* Winter (1991).

Lakonishok, Josef, Robert Vishny, and Andrei Shleifer. "Contrarian Investment: Extrapolation and Risk," Working Paper no. 4360. National Bureau of Economic Research, May, 1993.

Levis, Mario. "Stock Market Anomalies." *Journal of Banking and Finance* (December, 1989).

Malkiel, Burton. *A Random Walk Down Wall Street* 7th ed. New York: W.W. Norton, 2000.

Oppenheimer, Henry. "Ben Graham's Net Current Asset Values." *Financial Analysts Journal* (November/December, 1986).

O'Shaughnessy, James. *What Works on Wall Street*. New York: McGraw-Hill, 1997.

Poterba, James, and Larry Summers. "Mean Reversion in Stock Prices, Evidence and Implications." *Journal of Financial Economics* (March, 1988).

Power, D. M., A. A. Lonie, and R. Lonie. "The Over-Reaction Effect—Some U.K. Evidence." *British Accounting Review* 27 (1991).

Sharpe, William F. "Likely Gains from Market Timing." *Financial Analysts Journal* (March/April, 1975).

Shiller, Robert. *Irrational Exuberance*. Princeton, NJ: Princeton University Press, 2000.

Siegel, Jeremy. *Stocks for the Long Run* 2nd ed. New York: McGraw-Hill, 1998.

Swedroe, Larry. *What Wall Street Doesn't Want You to Know*. New York: St. Martin's Press, 2000.

Swensen, David. *Pioneering Portfolio Management*. New York: Free Press, 2000.

Tweedy, Brown & Company. "What Has Worked in Investing." Author, 1992.

Wright, Stephen, and Andrew Smithers. *Valuing Wall Street*. New York: McGraw-Hill, 2000.

Index

A

Abelson, Alan, 163
Adjusted for inflation, 12
Arnott, Robert, 56
Asness, Cliff, 56
Asset allocation, 149–150

B

Basu, Sanjoy, 33
Bernstein, William J., 3,
     150
Beta, 129
Bogle, John, 3, 55
Bond market yield, 85
Bonds, 89–94, 142–144
Book value, 71
Buffett, Warren, 8, 33, 137,
     176
Burns, Scott, 142
Buy low, 139

C

Cash, diversification, 140
Coca Cola, 72
Combined factors,
     111–114

Contrarian investment
     philosophy, 19
Coupon yields, 94
Cowles, 146

D

Danko, 35
DeBondt, Werner, 14, 73
Dimson, Elroy, 34, 185
Disney, Walt, 72
Diversification, 148
Diversify, 139–159
     asset allocation, 149–150
     bonds, 142–144
     cash, 140
     portfolio rebalancing,
          150–153
     real estate, 140–142
     stocks, 144–149
     timing costs, 153–159
Dividends, 50, 53–67
Dividend yield, 7, 50, 54–67,
     71, 105
Dollar cost averaging, 64–67,
     82–85
     based on market price,
          24–26
     using P/E ratio, 43–50
Donlan, Tom, 163